Personality and Politics

The Dickenson Series in Political Science
Edited by John C. Bollens, University of California, Los Angeles

Public Administration
John C. Buechner, University of Colorado

Legislatures in the American Political System
Dean E. Mann, University of California, Santa Barbara

American Foreign Policy in a Polycentric World
Douglas Mendel, University of Wisconsin — Milwaukee

Executives in the American Political System
John C. Ries, University of California, Los Angeles

State and Local Government and Politics
Gerald Rigby, University of Southern California

Courts in the American Political System
Henry J. Schmandt, University of Wisconsin — Milwaukee

Politics: Interest Group Theory
Harry M. Scoble, University of California, Los Angeles

American Political Thought
Duane E. Smith, University of California, Los Angeles

The Current International System
David O. Wilkinson, University of California, Los Angeles

Personality and Politics
E. Victor Wolfenstein, University of California, Los Angeles

Personality and Politics

E. Victor Wolfenstein

University of California, Los Angeles

Dickenson Publishing Company, Inc., Belmont, California

Library of Congress Catalog Card No.: 74-78886
Printed in the United States of America

To the memory of Robert F. Kennedy

Contents

5. CONCLUSION   *99*

Foreword

The books in THE DICKENSON SERIES IN POLITICAL SCIENCE are designed for use together or individually as texts or collateral readings. Each volume, prepared by a knowledgeable scholar, deals with a significant area of political science in a comprehensive, up-to-date, but concise manner. Each seeks to present a meaningful, stimulating analysis, not mere description, and is written in a direct, interesting style intended to inform rather than mystify. A bibliographical essay, which furnishes perspective and guidance for further reading in the field, constitutes an appropriate concluding section.

In *Personality and Politics*, E. Victor Wolfenstein offers a systematic examination of the implications of psychoanalytic theory for political life. Building on the work of Freud, Lasswell, Erikson, and others, he provides a lucid outline of psychoanalytic concepts needed for psychopolitical work. He considers Winston Churchill, Malcolm X, and Friedrich Nietzsche, three different types of political men—leader, adherent, and philosopher—and through the author's methods of inquiry, the reader is led to think psychoanalytically about the three of them, individually and comparatively.

This is a pioneering book and a welcome addition to the series.

Los Angeles, California   John C. Bollens

Preface

This book is primarily a psychological analysis of three political men, Winston Churchill, Malcolm X, and Friedrich Nietzsche. It is secondarily a study of three *types* of political men, the leader, the adherent, and the philosopher. Originally, my emphasis was exactly reversed. I planned a detailed inquiry into the typologies that have been and are used in psycho-political work. Increasingly, however, I found I learned more from studies that emphasized the application of a general theoretical perspective, especially psychoanalytic theory, to an individual case. The various categories, by contrast, seemed to fade into each other, sometimes even creating problems of understanding where none previously existed.

The question of what kinds of men perform what kinds of political actions cannot, of course, be entirely avoided—any more than one can operate clinically without some diagnostic categories. Even rough answers to questions such as what kinds of life experiences incline men toward leadership or creating philosophies help us to *begin* understanding human nature in politics. They are only a beginning, however, and cannot replace detailed study of individual cases.

In a book of this size it is not possible to produce a full analysis of a man's life. Yet I hope that, by following the application of psychoanalytic theory to the lives of these men, the reader will gain a sense of how to think psychoanalytically. It is this mode of thought, rather than any particular hypothesis, which is of central concern. Ideally, in fact, the reader will familiarize himself with *The Autobiography of Malcolm X* and the other sources so that he can think along with, and respond critically to, what is presented here.

I suspect that most readers, insofar as they react at all, will disagree with this study in one way or another. Hopefully this will not be in the form of an a priori rejection of psycho-political studies, but rather will represent an honest confrontation between their thoughts about these men and mine. Such an involvement would be the only real justification for this book, or, if the truth be told, for any book.

In a way, it is this kind of confrontation and involvement that produced the book. Discussions of Malcolm X and Winston Churchill with the Los Angeles Interdisciplinary Study Group, of Nietzsche with my students and friends, and of the three men in general with Dr. Martha Wolfenstein generated most of the ideas that are to be found here. Additionally, the editorial guidance of John Bollens not only helped to refine the manuscript, but ensured its completion.

Finally, it should be made clear that I admire deeply each of the men studied here. In trying to understand them, I am not in any sense devaluing their lives or their achievements. While not always agreeing with what they said and did, I have learned from each of them and hope others will also.

E.V.W.

Personality and Politics

1

Human Nature in Politics

Personality and Politics

This book is devoted to one general question: What are the relationships between a man's personality and his political behavior? We will explore the question by trying to think psychoanalytically about the lives of three men: Winston S. Churchill, a political leader; Malcolm X, a political adherent; and Friedrich Nietzsche, a political philosopher.

Let us, however, begin by following Nietzsche's advice to question the question itself: Why are we interested in marrying personality to politics? What reason do we have for thinking the union would be fruitful? The basis for this supposition is actually quite obvious. As Aristotle recognized, "man is by nature an animal intended to live in a polis." [1] Because man, for all his individuality, is a social being, we cannot understand his nature without understanding the social and political institutions that he uses, well or poorly, to structure and safeguard his existence. At the same time, we cannot make much sense of these institutions and social practices without knowing something about human psychology; for politics does not exist without individual men anymore than men exist without politics. In the words of John Stuart Mill:

The laws of the phenomena of society are, and can be, nothing but the laws of the actions and passions of human beings united together in the social state. Men, however, in a state of society, are still men; their actions and passions are obedient to the laws of individual human nature. [2]

[1] Ernest Barker, trans., *The Politics of Aristotle* (New York: Oxford University Press, 1958), p. 5.

[2] John Stuart Mill, *A System of Logic* (London: Longmans, Green & Co., Ltd., 1961), p. 573.

1

It would thus seem worthwhile to follow Graham Wallas in seeking an understanding of "human nature in politics." [3]

But what is human nature? Psychologically, what kind of creature is man? Throughout history, philosophers and students of politics have concerned themselves with this question without arriving at any generally accepted perspective.[4] A standard contemporary textbook, for example, discusses a dozen types of personality theory.[5] And if one added to these a goodly sampling of the theories of human nature that are no longer accepted, the list would grow to truly startling proportions.

This rich diversity of theory and opinion reflects the complexity of man himself. Indeed, human beings so defy conclusive analysis that one can often argue cogently quite opposing positions. Take for instance the views of John Locke and C. G. Jung on the relationship between personal identity and consciousness. According to Locke,

It is by the consciousness [a self] has of its present thoughts and actions that it is *self to itself* now, and so will be the same self, as far as the same consciousness can extend to actions past and to come. . . .[6]

Locke's view, one very much in the tradition of Descartes' "I think, therefore I am" and Thomas Hobbes' physics of the mind in the *Leviathan*, is that conscious reflection enables us to be sure of and to understand our individual natures. Yet, if one accepts the idea that man's mind continues to function even when he is not conscious, then one can posit as Jung does that

it transcends our powers of imagination to form a clear picture of what we are as a self, for in this operation the part would have to comprehend the whole. There is little hope of our ever being able to reach even approximate consciousness of the self, since however much we may make conscious there will always exist an indeterminate and indeterminable amount of unconscious material which belongs to the totality of the self.[7]

[3] Graham Wallas, *Human Nature in Politics* (London: Constable and Co., Ltd., 1948).

[4] The creation of psychology as a field truly distinct from other disciplines, with all the gains and losses that entails, did not occur until the latter part of the nineteenth century.

[5] Calvin S. Hall and Gardner Lindzey, *Theories of Personality* (New York: John Wiley & Sons, Inc., 1957).

[6] John Locke, *An Essay Concerning Human Understanding* (London: Oxford University Press, 1964), p. 189.

[7] C. G. Jung, "The Relations between the Ego and the Unconscious," in *Two Essays on Analytical Psychology* (New York: The World Publishing Company, 1956), pp. 186–187.

What is the role of consciousness in human nature? How important is it? In what sense are we or are we not defined by what we bring into consciousness? To these fundamental questions there are no universally agreed-upon answers.

Or take another basic issue, the nature of conscience and morality. One might want to agree with Mill that man is

a being capable of pursuing spiritual perfection as an end; of desiring, for its own sake, the conformity of his own character to his standard of excellence, without hope of good or fear of evil from other source than his own inward consciousness.[8]

But must one then disagree with Friedrich Nietzsche when he claims that man is "the sick animal," [9] a creature whose morality reflects his alienation from himself:

Man, with his need for self-torture, his sublimated cruelty resulting from the cooping up of his animal nature within a polity, invented bad conscience in order to hurt himself, after the blocking of the more natural outlet of his cruelty. Then this guilt-ridden man seized upon religion in order to exacerbate his self-torment to the utmost.[10]

Is morality man's highest natural motive, or a perversion of his natural motives? Both positions have been argued, and in the above example by men who were virtually contemporaries.

Perhaps, then, we ought to abandon our hope of linking human nature and politics? It would seem that human nature itself is so ambiguous that the attempt would be certain to end inconclusively. Indeed, this is the case. Any study of personality and politics will be, to a greater or lesser extent, tentative. Inquiries that do not attempt to reckon with human nature may appear to be more conclusive, but such clarity is likely to be deceptive. For whether we like it or not, politics is a human endeavor; and as a consequence, our understanding of it can be no more assured than our understanding of man himself. In directing our attention to personality and politics, we are not so much introducing a new variable or consideration as making manifest one that is always latent in political analysis.

We are, it is true, going to be treating personality and politics in a

[8] Mill, *On Bentham and Coleridge* (New York: Harper and Brothers, 1950), p. 66.

[9] Friedrich Nietzsche, *The Genealogy of Morals* (Garden City, New York: Doubleday & Company, Inc., 1956), p. 257.

[10] *Ibid.,* pp. 225–226.

certain way, a way indicated by the definitions assigned to the terms themselves: [11]

Political activity is any activity predominantly oriented to power and authority, with power defined as the *ability* to alter human behavior and authority as the *right* to alter it.[12]

A *personality* is a relatively stable organization of the ways in which an individual responds to his drives and intrapsychic demands, on the one hand, and his involvements in and conflicts with external reality, on the other.[13]

We are thus taking a broad view of politics and, as mentioned earlier, a psychoanalytic or "deep" view of personality. Both perspectives lead us to concentrate primarily on individual political participants rather than on types of participants or on aggregate data.

Our definition of politics leads us away from thinking about types of participants because it carries the implication that there is something political in human nature itself. It recognizes that each of us is, more or less fundamentally, concerned with questions of power and authority. We thus give up the (at least apparent) clarity that comes from saying that politics is activity connected with the formal institutions of government. We surrender, at the same time, any simple faith in generalizations about "political man" or types of political men; for, if men are only more or less political, then such generalizations can only more or less apply in any individual instance. Hence in this study more attention is paid to Churchill, Malcolm X, and Nietzsche than to leaders, adherents, or philosophers as such. Generalizations about political man and the varieties thereof are used to frame the individual studies, to faciliate comparison and analysis in much the same way that Weberian ideal types aid in the comparison of one society with another.[14] They may readily be put aside when more useful or interesting hypotheses are developed; and, what is more important, such typological propositions are no substitute for intensive analysis of particular cases.

Psychoanalytic theory, by emphasizing the complexity of man's

---

[11] There are, to be sure, many ways of defining these terms; but, as Humpty-Dumpty tells Alice, "When I use a word, it means just what I choose it to mean—neither more nor less."

[12] This definition is a modification of the one used by Marion J. Levy, Jr., as in his "Some Aspects of 'Structural-Functional' Analysis and Political Science," in Roland Young, ed., *Approaches to the Study of Politics* (Evanston, Ill.: Northwestern University Press, 1958).

[13] See one application of this usage in E. Victor Wolfenstein, *The Revolutionary Personality* (Princeton, N.J.: Princeton University Press, 1967).

[14] Cf. Max Weber, *The Methodology of the Social Sciences* (New York: Free Press of Glencoe, 1949).

psychic life, also directs our attention toward the individual. It requires that we look for the latent as well as the manifest meanings of actions; that we analyze the interaction of emotion, reason, and moral judgment when attempting to explain human behavior; and that we take seriously the often cited but seldom understood statement that "the child is father to the man." It stresses, moreover, the contradictions and ambivalences of our emotions. The goal of our inquiry accordingly is not the production of hypotheses that can easily be put into quantifiably testable form. Such hypotheses are, needless to say, valuable, as is the accumulation of the aggregate data needed for testing them.[15] Our goal, however, is a more modest one, a tentative understanding of the motivations of three men, and of the types of political men they embody and represent.

Two basic methods of inquiry will help us gain such an understanding: we will think psychoanalytically about each man, and we will compare the men with each other. More concretely in Chapter 2 several characteristics of the leader are enumerated, and the particular qualities Churchill brought to the role of leader are discussed. Then a psychological explanation of these qualities is sought through an analysis of Churchill's early life and the construction of a model of his adult personality. This model takes the form of a set of hypotheses about political leaders in general.

The chapters about Malcolm X and Nietzsche are similar in form to the one about Churchill. In each of these chapters, however, comparisons with Churchill are made, enabling us to gain some sense of the ways in which the men differ from and resemble each other. The resulting typological distinctions, as mentioned earlier, are to be taken only as rough approximations of a more complex reality in which leaders are sometimes philosophers and adherents often lead.

Some Elements of Psychoanalytic Theory

Because this study is devoted to what is usually called applied psychoanalysis (that is, the application of psychoanalytic theory to non-clinical material), it will be useful to indicate some of the basic elements of the theory.[16]

---

[15] Robert Lane in *Political Life* (New York: The Free Press, 1961) and Lane and David O. Sears in *Public Opinion* (Englewood Cliffs, N.J.: Prentice-Hall, Inc., 1964), analyze much of the broader body of psychopolitical literature.

[16] For more extensive introductions to psychoanalytic theory, see Otto Fenichel, *The Psychoanalytic Theory of Neurosis* (New York: W. W. Norton & Company, Inc., 1945); Sigmund Freud, *Introductory Lectures on Psychoanalysis* and *New Introductory Lectures on Psychoanalysis* in *The Standard Edition*

As a way of orienting ourselves to psychoanalysis, we might bring to mind certain affinities it has with Platonic thought. Like Plato's dialectic, psychoanalysis is essentially an unmasking process. Both Plato and Freud assumed that things may not always be as they appear, that the outward or apparent form of an object, thought, or mental process may serve to mask some underlying force or reality. Operating from this assumption, both men found dreams interesting, for dreams seemed to be a manifestation of a state of mind between normal consciousness and total oblivion, a state of mind that permitted the expression of normally concealed thoughts and wishes.

Both men, further, linked dreams to the irrational side of man's nature, and both saw sexual and aggressive impulses involved in man's irrationality:

[In our dreams] the wild beast in us ... becomes rampant and shakes off sleep to go in quest of what will gratify its own instincts. ... [It] will cast away all shame and prudence at such moments and stick at nothing. In phantasy it will not shrink from intercourse with a mother or anyone else, man, god or brute, or from forbidden food or any deed of blood.[17]

This passage from *The Republic* underlies Socrates' contention that a despotic man is one who "has become for all his waking life the man he used to be from time to time in his dreams." [18] It might just as easily have come from Freud's *The Interpretation of Dreams*.

Freud shared with Plato not only an interest in what is latent and hard to see in human nature, but also a preference for introspection and verbalization as tools for understanding the human mind. Freud's emphasis on free association (relaxing the mind so that thoughts come to consciousness without our normal degree of control or censorship) and dream analysis as ways of achieving self-knowledge does, of course, differ from Plato's faith in the dialectic of reason and sophistic discourse. Nonetheless, both are part of a common tradition in psychology which sees man's reason endangered by his inherent lack of reasonableness, his consciousness surrounded by an amorphous intrapsychic unconsciousness, and self-knowledge as something unvarnished goodwill and observation are insufficient to achieve.

---

of the Complete Works of Sigmund Freud (Hereafter cited as *Standard Ed.*) (London: Hogarth Press, 1964), vols. 15–16 and 22; or, for a more compact introduction, Calvin S. Hall, *A Primer of Freudian Psychology* (New York: Mentor Books, 1964).

[17] F. M. Cornford, trans., *The Republic of Plato* (New York: Oxford University Press, 1945), p. 296.

[18] *Ibid.,* p. 300.

As noted in the previous section, we have defined "personality" in such a way as to make it compatible with this way of thinking. It posits no simple, unitary self; rather man is seen as often internally divided, trying to manage both his inner needs and his interactions with the people in his environment. In psychoanalytic theory, as in most theories of human nature, reason is given a major role in performing this function. Even Freud's ultimate therapeutic and cultural injunction, "where there was id, there ego shall be," bespeaks the desire to replace what is irrational and instinctual in man with self-consciousness and rationality.[19] But psychoanalysis, while recognizing reason as a basic attribute of man, sees its task as complex and hazardous. Man must use his reason to learn when to and when not to gratify his sexual, aggressive, and other drives, with what objects and in what ways; to test the requirements of his environment for survival; to respond to the moral imperatives of his own conscience and his society; and to integrate all of these functions so that they do not interfere too radically with each other.[20]

This complex process, moreover, is only partially conscious. Indeed, according to psychoanalytic theory, many of our thoughts and desires never become conscious, or many be driven from consciousness without leaving a visible trace. A brief look at psychosexual maturation will serve to clarify the point.

The process of character formation begins at birth, if not before, and is largely completed by the end of adolescence. Man thus matures emotionally over a long period of time. As Erik Erikson puts it,

It is human to have a long childhood; it is civilized to have an even longer childhood. Long childhood makes a technical and mental virtuoso out of man, but it also leaves a lifetime residue of emotional immaturity in him.[21]

The experiences and desires of early childhood live on in each of us. Even the oral phase, roughly the first year of life, influences our adult behavior. Depending on the relative presence or absence of maternal warmth and comfort at this time, we will be more or less trusting—of ourselves and others—in our adult actions.

[19] Freud, *New Introductory Lectures . . . (Standard Ed.,* 22), p. 80.

[20] The *ego* is the structural concept used in psychoanalytic theory to indicate the part of the personality in terms of which the functions of reality-testing, impulse-gratification, and psychic integration are performed. The *id* is used to denote the source of the drives, of psychic energy; and the *superego,* for the psychic structure in terms of which moral functions are performed.

[21] Erik H. Erikson, *Childhood and Society* (New York: John Wiley & Sons, Inc., 1963), p. 12.

The mother's influence continues to dominate in the next phase, for the chances are very great that she will be primarily involved in the child's toilet training. Toilet training, at least in western cultures, is usually an early testing ground of a child's independence and autonomy. Control over urinary and defecatory functions, as well as the rudiments of a more general restraint, are at issue in the interaction of mother and child. A warm and skillful mother, with a trusting child, will together create situations in which the child feels that his control over his body and his behavior, his effort to be clean, is, to a great extent, his own prerogative. He will cooperate with his mother out of love and self-pride, not out of fear and shame. Self-confidence and realistic self-control are thus the favorable outcomes of this phase; pervasive feelings of uncertainty, and a need for (although fear of) rigid control result from an anal phase that is punitive and overly demanding.

There are two general ways in which the experiences of even these earliest phases may influence adult attitudes. First, the predispositions developed at this time may be reinforced by the experiences of subsequent periods. A cheerful child will be more likely to get loving responses from others than a morose one, so that his optimism may create, in the form of happy experiences, its own justification. It is always possible, of course, for life circumstances to alter radically, as we will see in each of the three examples discussed; but, everything else being equal, early predispositions tend to act as self-fulfilling prophecies.

Second, the ungratified impulses of these as well as later phases may be *repressed*, driven or kept from consciousness and from access to discharge. The child learns that some of his desires are unacceptable to his parents. As his own conscience develops, they become unacceptable to him as well. Thus, in order not to lose the love of his parents and suffer the reproaches of his conscience, he must either repress these desires or find socially acceptable ways of gratifying them. In either event they will continue to exist and to influence his behavior, despite the fact that he may have no conscious knowledge of the impulses in their original form.[22]

The genital or oedipal phase, which comes between the ages of three and six, culminates in a major substitution of intrapsychic constraints on impulse for the direct control of the parents: conscience increasingly comes to supplement parental authority. Correspondingly, there is an increased use of repression as a defense

---

[22] Repression is the most basic of the defense mechanisms, the techniques the ego uses in warding off and sometimes discharging unwelcome impulses.

against unacceptable desires. At this age a child is more aware of genital sensations than he has previously been; and this awareness is combined with a greater interest in and understanding of the intimacy that his parents share. The male child feels himself, consciously or unconsciously, sexually attracted to his mother; he perceives, moreover, that sexual contact with his mother is precluded by his father's relationship to her. His father's privileged position hence draws his hostility, while his love for and fear of his father prevents the full expression of this resentment. In other words, the son's feelings for his father are intensely *ambivalent*, an ambiguous and conflicting mixture of love and hate.

To reduce this ambivalence, the young boy takes into his mind a punitive image of his father. The resulting *identification* with his father is one of the primary bases of conscience; the internalized image of the father produces feelings of guilt and anxiety whenever parricidal or incestuous wishes approach consciousness.[23] Guilt and ambivalence arc then relieved by the repression of the forbidden impulses. Under favorable circumstances, the feelings of guilt and the resultant repression are moderate. Conscience, an internalized sense of right and wrong, develops without gross exaggeration or harshness. The child retains a feeling of his own worth and goodness limited by an increased sensitivity to the rights of others. Under less favorable conditions, dutiful and unquestioning submission to a punitive set of moral standards or unreasoning rebellion against any restraint are also possible outcomes of this phase.

In any event, the strains of the genital phase, as well as a slowing of physical maturation, usually lead to a reduced level of drive expression over the next few years. Especially boys shun relations with members of the opposite sex, preferring to solidify the identification with the father begun during the previous phase in ways that do not threaten to reopen old wounds. Boys emulate their fathers by learning skills, by becoming good students or good athletes. They do not compete with their fathers by seeking intimacy with either their mothers or girls their own age, but rather by strengthening their ties to other boys.

The latency period, as it is called, ends with the onset of puberty, roughly between the twelfth and the fourteenth year. At this time, the existing psychic balance tends to be overthrown. Personality integration at the latency level is predicated upon the repression of drives of a certain intensity. With the physiological maturation of

[23] More generally, an identification is any internalization of an aspect of another person.

adolescence, more intense feelings and impulses emerge, so that the old patterns of impulse control become inadequate. The long-repressed conflicts of early childhood again approach consciousness. Now, however, they are combined with the greater sexual and aggressive possibilities of incipient manhood. The resulting ambivalence is often sufficiently intense to necessitate the separation of a young man from the parents, especially the father, he both loves and hates.

Viewed from another perspective, adolescence presents the challenge of finding a social role, including both an occupation and patterns of emotional involvement with peers, which allows a person to maintain an adequate level of psychic integration. Thus if a person chooses politics as a vocation, it is likely that a political career seems to promise him emotional expression combined with the ability to control the intrapsychic and interpersonal conflicts of adolescence and young manhood.

It should be noted that adolescence is defined not only by physical maturation but by social norms and individual circumstances as well. For some young men personality development comes to a conclusive halt with the end of their formal education; for others a period of groping extending over many years may precede the final establishment of a satisfactory mode of work and of love. Churchill was settled in a political-military career during his early twenties; Malcolm X was changing in important ways when he died at thirty-nine; and Nietzsche's life was greatly altered after he left the University of Basel when he was about thirty-five. Yet even the relatively late changes in the life patterns of the latter two men are continuous with, and understandable in terms of, their early experiences. Or, to put it another way, each of these men is recognizably himself even before, but certainly during, adolescence.

Part of the recognizability of any personality stems from the use of characteristic means of defense against impulse. We have already mentioned repression and identification as two of the ways in which an unwanted desire may be checked and kept from consciousness. Three other means of defense are important for an understanding of the men we are studying.

One way of circumventing a repression, of releasing an impulse which is unacceptable to the conscious mind, is to change the object of the drive. Thus one might *displace* a feeling of antagonism from a parent, whom one is commanded to love, to a toy that may safely be destroyed, a movie villain whom one may hate, or a school administrator who stands *in loco parentis*. Against such a surrogate object hostility can be expressed without the guilt that accompanies it within the family. Sexual drives can, of course, be similarly displaced.

A repressed impulse may also be *projected* onto another object. Another person or thing is perceived as having an attribute that more properly belongs to the self. The lover who feels that everybody loves him is a familiar embodiment of this way of channeling emotion, as is the man who, without evidence, feels that everybody hates him. Needless to say, there are less extreme uses of this defense.

Finally, a web of *rationalization* may be spun around an impulse, act, or feeling to make its underlying character obscure to both the self and others. Thus feelings of disappointment are masked by deciding that one did not want it anyhow, or acts of aggression may be justified by coming to believe that one had no choice.

Each of these ways of defending against and releasing emotion may be used more or less intensively, and more or less consciously. They may also be used singly or in combination. Short of extreme mental illness, they do not replace realistic perception of the environment or more direct forms of emotional gratification. Thus, in discussing Churchill, Malcolm X, and Nietzsche, the use of these and other psychoanalytic concepts does not imply that the men were either neurotic or psychotic.[24]

A final word of caution before we turn to Churchill's political career. There is always a danger in psychological studies that explanation will be mistaken for evaluation. This book attempts to explain certain aspects of three men's behavior; it does not sit in judgment of either the men or their actions. This is not to say, however, that the study is completely objective. Clearly my values and scientific biases influence both the presentation of the data and its interpretation; but the intent of the book is to examine human nature in politics, not to applaud or belittle it.

---

[24] Nietzsche did in fact become insane some years before his death; but his madness will not be of direct concern to us.

2

Political Leaders

All human beings have something in common, yet no two people are exactly alike. This double truth ensures that all attempts to classify men, such as the well-known, if equally ill-defined, clinical categories of man as healthy, neurotic, or psychotic will involve a degree of distortion and ambiguity; for no typology can convey the full complexity of an individual life, no category can preserve a sense of the unique quality of any man's existence. Hence, someone like Kafka's protagonist in *The Trial*. Joseph K., is a distinct and living character. Reduced to a case of paranoia, he loses the subtlety that gave him life and crumbles before our eyes into an inert heap of attributes or traits. Yet the concept "paranoid psychosis" does help us to understand Joseph K., just as a freeway map helps us to find our way in Los Angeles.

Unlike road maps, however, which permit us easily to distinguish one street from another, psychological maps have an awkward way of being blurred and hard to read. A perfectly healthy man, for example, may find himself behaving in a psychotic fashion in his dreams. Or, to put it another way, we can find qualities that are markedly present in the waking life of psychotics in the dreams of a normal man; what differentiates the one from the other is the relative importance of, and balance among, the traits that comprise the personality. Such matters of quantity and interrelationship are, unfortunately, difficult to measure or depict. Consequently typologies based on, say, the degree of reality testing, or the relative amounts of reality testing and defensive responding do not permit us to place men unambiguously into one or another category. The psychologist as scientific classifier can, therefore, provide nothing more than the starting point for the psychologist as artist of the individual psyche.

Winston Churchill as Political Leader:
"We Shall Fight . . . "

Keeping the above limitations in mind, let us admit that experienced observers can distinguish, for example, between men with "judicial temperaments" and those who are of "presidential caliber," or between those who are good administrators and those who are good orators. Similarly, we can indicate several of the manifest personality traits of men who are successful political leaders. Winston Churchill, as indicated in Chapter 1, will be used to exemplify these generalizations, and to provide the basis for the hypotheses about leaders developed later in the chapter.

Most basically, like all men who are active in politics, those who strive for positions of leadership are vitally concerned with power and authority. They desire and relish the strength, the force, required to achieve their goals; and they crave a feeling of rectitude or legitimacy for themselves and the cause they serve. The more a man desires and is able to play the role of leader, the more he will have a sense of his own power and the righteousness of his cause, and the more he will feel that he is the only one who fully understands what course of action any given situation demands. Thus Churchill, called to the Prime Ministership of England in the dark and dangerous spring of 1940, felt confident of his ability to lead his country in her conflict with Nazi Germany. In his account of World War II, he describes his feelings as he prepared for bed at the end of the long day on which he had assumed his awesome responsibilities:

But I cannot conceal from the reader of this truthful account that as I went to bed at about 3 A.M., I was conscious of a profound sense of relief. At last I had the authority to give directions over the whole scene. I felt as if I were walking with Destiny, and that all my past life had been but a preparation for this hour and this trial. . . . I thought I knew a good deal about [the situation], and I was sure I should not fail. Therefore, although impatient for the morning, I slept soundly and had no need for cheering dreams. Facts are better than dreams.[1]

It might be added that the situation Churchill found himself in was the realization of a lifelong dream, a dream of combined military and political glory. Having gained the office he sought for almost half a century, Churchill savored the power and authority of his position.

A second characteristic of the leader is that he keeps his eyes

[1] Winston S. Churchill, *The Gathering Storm* (Boston: Houghton Mifflin Company, 1948), p. 667.

fixed firmly on his political goals. He devotes virtually all of his typically enormous energies to gaining his end, be it the overthrow of
an existing regime, as in the case of the revolutionist, or the attain-
ment of high office, as in the case of the nonrevolutionary politician.
Churchill decided that he wanted a political career, and ultimately
the highest office in the land (excluding the Crown, of course), when
he was a schoolboy at Harrow. For reasons that will become apparent
later, he was not able to approach his goal directly; and, from the
time he was twenty-one until he was twenty-four, he was a subaltern
in the British cavalry. Stationed in India in 1896, he did not accept
the pleasant and rather indolent life an officer there could easily lead.
Rather, he sought out situations of military conflict and succeeded
in getting himself reassigned to the commands involved. Although
stationed in southern India, he managed to fight not only in the
northwest frontier engagements, but even in Lord Kitchener's Nile
River campaign of 1898. It took extraordinary perserverence and gall,
to say nothing of family connections, for Churchill to win such far-
ranging assignments.

His purpose in this sustained effort was to gain military glory, and
by so doing a reputation that would carry him into the House of
Commons. His earliest letters to his mother from India are rich in
references to what he would be doing if he were in the House. When
his newspaper reports of the Indian frontier appeared in print un-
signed, he was unhappy because he had hoped they would "bring
[his] personality before the electorate." [2] And throughout his military
career Churchill read widely, especially in the parlimentary records,
to prepare himself for his political career. Finally, when he was
elected to the House in 1900, just before his twenty-sixth birthday,
he devoted himself to political advancement just as assiduously as
he had applied himself to getting elected.

Another attribute of the leader is that, in his drive to gain personal ascendancy or the victory of his cause, he is willing to sacrifice
the ambitions and even the lives of other men, and to break the bonds
of personal friendship if policy should so dictate. Churchill, who
switched party affiliation twice in his career (first from Conservative
to Liberal, then back from Liberal to Conservative), broke with most
of his friends in politics in one move or the other. And, on another
front, he unhesitatingly gave orders, as First Lord of the Admiralty
during World War I and as Prime Minister during World War II,

[2] Randolph S. Churchill, *Winston S. Churchill: Youth* (Boston: Houghton
Mifflin Company, 1966), p. 343. From a letter from Winston Churchill to his
mother dated October 25, 1897.

which resulted in massive losses of human life. (He was, of course, equally willing to place his own life in jeopardy.)

The willingness of the leader to give up the assurance of lasting ties is closely related to the often-noted loneliness, or, perhaps more accurately, aloneness, of high office, for the leader is a man who, by definition, has no equal, and certainly no superior. He senses himself to be a man apart, and a man above; his destiny or his deity does not allow him simple companionship with other men. Churchill's novel *Savrola*, written while he was stationed in India, makes the point clearly,[3] for the titular character, a young politician who is obviously an idealization of Churchill himself, radiates an aura of command which gains him respect but not intimacy, admirers but not peers, success but not tranquility. Savrola easily wins followers for his cause, for his political, and ultimately armed, attack on the tyrannical president of the fictional state of Laurania; but his closest friend is killed in the fight for freedom, and Savrola himself is almost forced to give up the woman he loves. (In the novel Churchill tacks on a happy ending which is even less believable than the story itself; but, as the final chorus of *The Threepenny Opera* tells us: "In real life the ending isn't quite so fine / The victorious messenger does not come riding often.")

Churchill's novel, for all its late Victorian romanticism, captures realistically one aspect of politics, and thus one aspect of political leaders. The Lauranian world is one of conflict, as is the real political world on which it was modeled. And leaders are adepts at the management, and often the accentuation, of conflict. They are only rarely men like Gandhi who are repelled by violence; and even the peace-loving Mahatma was involved in political competition in which violence and aggression were never far from the surface and often broke through. Churchill's involvement with violence is perhaps the most striking aspect of his political career.

Churchill's political style was distinctive both for its content and its constancy. He unfailingly viewed politics as a form of military campaigning, and military action as a way of achieving political goals. We have already seen that political ambition underlay his active military career; but it was his military outlook that led him to besiege two anarchists who were barricaded in a house on Sidney Street in London with over seven hundred and fifty police, several soldiers, and a Maxim gun when he was Home Secretary in 1911. The result of this escapade was, not surprisingly, public ridicule and a temporary loss of prestige.[4]

[3] Winston S. Churchill, *Savrola: A Tale of Revolution in Laurania* (New York: Longmans, Green & Co., 1900).

[4] For a full account of this incident, see Peter de Mendelssohn, *The Age of Churchill* (London: Thames & Hudson, 1961), I, 502–507.

This same outlook led him to fight for an enlarged British navy during the months preceding World War I, and to see in the German glider clubs of the 1930s the renascence of the German air force. He was his government's harshest critic in the years preceding the outbreak of hostilities between Germany and England in 1939, and its most effective spokesman when he became its leader. Defiantly facing the apparently impregnable German army, his war cry inspired his nation—and ours:

We shall go on to the end, we shall fight in France, we shall fight on the seas and oceans, we shall fight with growing confidence and growing strength in the air, we shall defend our island, whatever the cost may be, we shall fight on the beaches, we shall fight on the landing grounds, we shall fight in the fields and in the streets, we shall fight in the hills; we shall never surrender. . . . [5]

After the fighting was over, after the glorious days of the Battle of Britain—her finest hour, as Churchill put it—the man who had led his nation to victory felt himself out of touch with the somber postwar world. As he said to his physician, Lord Moran: "I have a strong feeling that my work is done. I have no message. I had a message. Now I can only say 'fight the damned socialists!' I do not believe in this brave new world." [6] But the early postwar years were a time of reconciliation, not of combat, and so in the electoral campaign of 1946 Churchill led his party to a resounding defeat.

Even this defeat, however, did not crush the man. He retained the leadership of the Conservative Party and, in the early years of the Cold War, again became Prime Minister. This resiliency points to another characteristic of leaders in general—that is, they are, psychologically and usually physically, strong men. Lenin's composure during the difficult days of 1917, Roosevelt's jaunty smile in 1932, de Gaulle's rallying of his people after the fall of France—these are the public manifestations of a strength of character great leaders display in their private lives as well. Not that men like Churchill are creatures of godlike serenity; indeed, quite the contrary: Churchill himself was notorious for his often-prolonged fits of melancholia. But great leaders are not permanently incapacitated by blows, public or private, which would destroy lesser men.

[5] Winston S. Churchill, *Blood, Sweat, and Tears* (New York: C. P. Putnam's Sons, 1941), p. 297. From Churchill's June 4, 1940 address to the House of Commons, following the evacuation of Dunkirk.

[6] Cited by Churchill's physician, Lord Moran, in his *Churchill* (Boston: Houghton Mifflin Company, 1966), p. 197.

On the manifest level, leaders gain strength, a sense of their own power and authority, through identification with their cause. Churchill thought of himself as a servant of the English nation; thus England's might, and England's right, were his to share. Characteristically, his motto for the English people, which he affixes to his account of World War II, concisely represents his personal credo as well, the credo of the politician as warrior, the warrior as politician:

> In War: Resolution
> In Defeat: Defiance
> In Victory: Magnanimity
> In Peace: Good Will

Our task, in the next section, is to come to an understanding of the psychogenesis of this attitude toward politics and the accompanying style of political action. In so doing, we may also hope to be in a position to explain the genesis and operation of the other qualities of leaders mentioned in the preceding pages.

Winston Churchill's Youth

Early Childhood

Winston Spencer Churchill was born on November 30, 1874. His father, Lord Randolph Churchill, was one of the leading young socialites of the period, and was soon to be one of its leading politicians. His mother, Jeanette Jerome Churchill, an American, was widely admired for her beauty and had a taste for elegance which was to be the virtual financial ruin of three husbands. Neither parent found much love or time to devote to Winston; for each, the social and political whirls were incomparably more interesting than a bumptious, energetic, and loving boy. Indeed, as Sir Winston's son puts it in his biography of his father, "The neglect and lack of interest in [my father] shown by his parents were remarkable, even judged by the standards of late Victorian and Edwardian days." [7]

The resulting loneliness and emotional isolation were fortunately relieved by the love and devotion of his nurse, Elizabeth Everest. "Woomany," as Winston and his younger brother Jack (born in 1880) called her, provided the mothering Lady Randolph was in-

---

[7] Randolph Churchill, *op. cit.,* p. 43.

capable of supplying. Her steady and unconditional affection provided Winston with a sense of his own value and goodness: she loved him for what he *was*, not for what he *did*, and thus gave Winston a mirror of feeling in which he appeared unfailingly lovable and admirable. Here we probably have the basis, aside from constitutional factors, of the very considerable self-esteem and confidence Winston possessed in later life. His relationship with his parents, by contrast, contributed a ceaseless striving after an all but unobtainable and strictly conditional love and recognition, on the one hand, and an equally fierce search for enemies to meet and conquer, on the other.

Although Winston yearned for the affection of both parents, it was his mother's love he most craved during his early years. When he was two years old, the family moved to Ireland, and it is from Ireland that he carried away his first memories:

My picture of [my mother] in Ireland is in a riding habit, fitting like a skin and often beautifully spotted with mud. She and my father hunted continually on their large horses; and sometimes there were great scares because one or the other did not come back for many hours after they were expected.
My mother always seemed to me a fairy princess; a radiant being possessed of limitless riches and power. . . .
My mother made a brilliant impression upon my childhood's eye. She shone for me like the Evening Star. I loved her dearly but at a distance.[8]

Longingly, anxiously, Winston waited for his mother to return to him from her rides, her very sensuously described rides, with his father. It is not difficult to surmise that such riding stands symbolically for the sexual intimacy of mother and father, and that Winston desired, but was not able to obtain, this intimacy for himself. Of course, almost no one, short of the legendary Oedipus himself, gains the realization of this childhood wish. For Winston, however, the disjunction between wish and reality was greater than usual. His mother's very remoteness served to magnify her charm, and to lessen those opportunities for normal affection and abrasion which help to transform parents, in their children's minds, from the most potent of gods and goddesses into human beings. Consequently, instead of perceiving his mother realistically as a woman with human failings, Winston viewed her, consciously as a child and unconsciously as an adult, as a princess, a queen.

Most men, it can be said, carry with them unconsciously a romanticized image of their mothers. This image influences their

8 Winston S. Churchill, *My Early Life: A Roving Commission* (New York: Charles Scribner's Sons, 1958), pp. 4–5.

search for a woman to love, and helps to explain their fascination with princesses and movie stars, the alluring heroines of novels and the liberally displayed femininity of *Playboy* magazine. At the same time, men unconsciously carry an exaggeratedly maternal picture of their mothers—mother as unfailingly loving, comforting, warming, and the like. To live in a satisfying way with a woman, a man must integrate these two images and moderate them, bringing them into accord with the realities of human nature.

For Churchill, such an integration was not possible. Practically from his birth, the romantic and maternal aspects of the mother were embodied in different women. Mrs. Everest gave him the maternal loving that any child craves, and in adult life his wife Clementine helped to nurture and care for him. Clementine was also, of course, an object of romantic interest; but neither she nor any other woman could live up to the image of romantic beauty Churchill carried in his mind. Not even Lady Randolph herself could, as the years passed, compete with herself as seen through admiring eyes of a five-year-old boy. In fact, Churchill learned to deal with his mother very realistically. He knew what he could expect from her, how to win her compliance to his wishes, and how to guide her, at least to some extent, along the road he wished her to travel. As a result, a replacement, a substitute, for Lady Randolph was needed, something that Churchill could love and serve as a knight errant serves his Arthurian princess.

The rhetoric of royalty, which Churchill himself uses in describing his mother, provides us with an indication of what Churchill came to love in place of his mother; for it was no great leap for a member of one of England's leading families to think of himself as a protector of the Crown (at that time worn by Queen Victoria) instead of a protector of his mother, a parliamentary suitor of the English nation instead of an amorous suitor of his "Evening Star." Thus Churchill's first notable intellectual feat was, at the age of fourteen, to memorize over one thousand lines from Macaulay's *Lays of Ancient Rome*, and to cherish especially those lines describing how brave Horatius defends his motherland:

> Then out spoke brave Horatius,
>   The Captain of the Gate:
> "To every man upon this earth
>   Death cometh soon or late.
> And how can man die better
>   Than facing fearful odds,
> For the ashes of his fathers,
>   And the temples of his Gods,

> And for the tender mother
>   Who dandled him to rest,
> And for the wife who nurses
>   His baby at her breast,
> And for the holy maidens
>   · Who feed the eternal flame,
> To save them from false Sextus
>   That wrought the deed of shame?" [9]

Horatius, of course, survives the onslaught of Rome's enemies and, although wounded, swims the Tiber in full armor after protecting his countrymen. In short, Churchill elected for himself Horatius' role, the role of triumphant defender and lover of the mother country. Our hypothesis is that he made this choice as a displacement from his idealized and unobtainable mother.

Horatius' speech also sums up nicely Churchill's feelings for his father: Horatius would defend "the ashes of his fathers / And the temples of his Gods." Churchill spent much of his political life defending his father's memory. Indeed, it is not too much to say that Churchill became his father in order to serve him all the better. But it was his father's memory that Churchill served, not his father; and in this fact lies the key to understanding the ambivalent and tormented relationship of Winston to Lord Randolph.

Ambivalence is, as we saw in Chapter 1, a usual aspect of human relations, and is especially common in the relationship between son and father. On the one hand, the son views the father as someone who rapes the mother, and who would attack him as well for defending the mother or attempting to gain sexual union with her. On the other hand, the father is loved by and loves the mother, is loved by and loves the son. The typical solution to this dilemma is to identify with the father, to use an internalized representation of the father to control the sexual impulse toward the mother and the hostile impulse toward the father.

We would infer that this emotional configuration was present in Churchill. His relationship to his father, however, like his relationship to his mother, was attenuated and distorted by parental coldness and lack of contact. Just as Winston had to work out his feelings for his mother at a distance, so he had to deal with an image of his father rather than with his father himself. In fact, the kind of emotional division which young Churchill established for coping with his relationship to his mother was used for his father as well. His father

---

[9] Lady Trevelyan, ed., *The Works of Lord Macaulay* (London: Longmans, Green & Co., 1866), p. 473.

was split into two components, one of them aggressive, dangerous, and evil, the other, loving, fair, and virtuous. The former attributes were given to virtually all men outside the Marlborough family, the latter traits were reserved for Lord Randolph and a few other men.

Thus, throughout his autobiography, Churchill is unfailing in his admiration and respect for his father, and in later life he tried mightily to emulate him; but his descriptions of the male world around him are pervaded by violence and aggression. Take, for example, his account of his life in Ireland. We are told of a theater manager who was killed in a fire: "All that was found of the manager was the keys that had been in his pocket." [10] Winston was disappointed when he was not permitted to see the keys. He remembers "a tall white tower . . . [that] had been blown up by Oliver Cromwell." [11] One day, when out for a ride, he reports that Mrs. Everest mistook the local rifle brigade for a group of Irish revolutionists. In the excitement of this event, Winston was thrown from the the donkey he was riding and received a concussion. And he remembers that a man who gave him a gift was later killed by real Irish revolutionists.[12]

Needless to say, these events did take place: but so did many other activities which Churchill either did not remember or did not see fit to record. This alertness to the violence around him was, throughout his life, one of Churchill's distinguishing characteristics. He would take even slight indications of hostility seriously, sometimes to his and his country's advantage, sometimes not. At the same time, he was very slow to see the hostility and lack of love that were his father's predominant attitudes toward him, and he was prone to overevaluate the qualities of those few men whom he allowed to get relatively close to him.

This dichotomous relationship to men, this treating of them as completely friend or completely foe, may be explained by supposing that, through lack of contact with his father, and fear of losing whatever affection his father gave him, Winston was forced to repress, to drive from consciousness, his aggressive impulses. Doing so allowed him a modicum of peace in his interaction with his father. It necessitated, however, finding alternative outlets for his aggression. Such outlets could be found by displacing the locus of conflict from self and family to self and world, and then projecting his own hostile impulses onto others. Thus Winston created for himself a dangerous, but familiar, world in which he was prone to see aggression where there

[10] Winston Churchill, *My Early Life,* p. 2.
[11] *Ibid.*
[12] *Ibid.*

was none and, at the same time, was able to combat it where it did exist. And he could feel that his own aggression was simply a reaction to the aggressive intent of others.

As may be seen from the memories Winston Churchill had of his sojourn in Ireland, his life was from the outset influenced by politics. Lord Randolph was already involved in parliamentary activity, which in part accounts for his lack of availability to his son; the violence that Churchill reports was often political violence; and Winston's grandfather, with whom he and his parents resided, was the Viceroy of Ireland. Churchill's position in life thus made it easy for him to use politics as an area for the displacement of emotion.

We are accordingly not surprised to find that Churchill's most vivid memory from the Irish period is of a political ceremony:

I remember my grandfather, the Viceroy, unveiling the Lord Gough statue in 1878. A great black crowd, scarlet soldiers on horseback, strings pulling away a brown shiny sheet, the old Duke, the formidable grandpapa, talking loudly to the crowd. I recall even a phrase he used: "and with a withering volley he shattered the enemy's line." I quite understood that he was speaking about war and fighting and that a "volley" meant what the black-coated soldiers (Riflemen) used to do with loud bangs so often in the Phoenix Park where I was taken for my morning walks.[13]

Initially, of course, we are struck by the continuity, both personal and familial, between Churchill's earliest experiences and his adult career. How often would he, like his grandfather, preside over a political ceremony commemorating a military event!

The event has another meaning scarcely less obvious than that already mentioned. Winston was impressed by the glorification of this man of violence. If we treat his recollection as a screen memory, as an event remembered because it permits the disguised representation of a forbidden impulse, then we see a young boy who wished for love and attention as his reward for performing an aggressive action, for "shattering the enemy." [14] The ceremony becomes a vehicle for expressing the oedipal wish just because it seemed to promise such a possibility. It was, after all, an unveiling, a revealing of something concealed. Its message, which Winston assuredly did not grasp at the time but which was reinforced and amplified in the years ahead,

---

[13] *Ibid.,* p. 1.

[14] Screen memories, like any indirect form of impulse gratification (such as neurotic symptoms, dreaming, creative writing, or political participation), are based on the displacement of emotion. The centrality of displacement to our understanding of man in general and political men in particular is accordingly already apparent.

was that, in politics, bold, active aggression would serve to annihilate the enemy and to win love and respect. Young Churchill, entering school for the first time in 1882, was thus predisposed to find enemies awaiting him and to face them boldly.

Before turning to Churchill's school days, it should be said that the interpretation presented thus far may not be correct; but it does fit the facts and is consonant with what we know about human nature in general. It helps us find, moreover, continuities between Churchill's childhood and his adult life, something any good psychogenetic inter- pretation must be able to do. Still we are not entitled to treat it as anything more than hypothetical, and must be willing to give it up either in favor of a more cogent argument or in the face of invalidat- ing evidence.

School Days

Fortunately or unfortunately, Winston's first public experience did little to modify the view of the world he had generated out of his interaction with his family. This was true in part because Winston entered school prepared to dislike it and to take exception to its rules and demands.[15] Just as importantly, however, Winston's first school was administered in a brutal fashion.

Saint George's School in Ascot, which, as we noted, Winston en- tered in 1882, was run by the Reverend H. W. Sneyd-Kynnersley. The school itself was strict and rather oppressive, a far cry from the un- disciplined life Winston had led under Mrs. Everest's gentle sur- veillance; but Sneyd-Kynnersley added a genuinely sadistic element to what was otherwise conventional public school cruelty. Churchill himself later noted that the floggings recalcitrant boys received (and none were more recalcitrant than he) "exceeded in severity anything that would have been tolerated in any of the Reformatories under the Home Office." [16] By the time Winston was taken out of the school two years later, when Mrs. Everest found welts and scars from his beatings, he had had ample opportunity to confirm his opinion that the world of men was a world of pain, and that male authority was punitive and dangerous.

Churchill's juxtaposition of the Home Office and Saint George's School is by no means fortuitous. By placing them side by side he is serving several emotional purposes. He is, first, telling his readers that

---

[15] Winston Churchill, *My Early Life,* p. 10.

[16] *Ibid.,* p. 12. It is important to note for the argument developed below that Churchill was himself Home Secretary in 1910–1911.

Saint George's was for him a prison, and a cruel one at that. It was, in other words, a place of punishment, an enforced exile from the people he loved. But for what was he being punished? Manifestly, to be sure, he was not being punished at all, but merely sent to school as a matter of course. Unconsciously, however, one might suppose that Winston felt he was being punished just because he felt guilty, guilty of loving his mother too much and his father too little.

Let us pause here to note that Winston's entire school career, before he entered Sandhurst Military Academy in 1893, was marked by disobedience to authority and slovenly work. He was constantly getting into trouble for one or another escapade or academic failing. Although he was manifestly contrite after each one, his persistence leads one to believe that he was gaining a degree of gratification from his actions. Indeed, his behavior strikingly resembles the actions of those whom Freud called criminals from a sense of guilt.[17] Such people act in a criminal manner in order simultaneously to admit and deny an unconscious feeling of guilt, to ward off the punishment of castration for their oedipal guilt by accepting a less terrifying punishment for a contemporary crime. If we treat Churchill's negligence in school as analogous to such criminality, then we would view it as an unconsciously devised compromise between open hostility toward the father and complete submission to him. Churchill loved his father too much, and was too afraid of his father's strength, actually to rebel. He also had too much pride and strength, too much defiance, to become a dutiful, unobtrusive schoolboy. Hence we may view him as striking a balance between the two poles, acting in such a way as to assert and deny his aggressive impulses, to accept and ward off punishment and feelings of guilt.

If such a construction of Churchill's school performance is correct, then it is a tribute to his character that he was able to maintain the balance as he did. Acceptance of one or the other of the polarities would have, in the long run, reduced considerably the feelings of ambivalence with which he had to live; but Winston clung tenaciously to this delicate juxtaposition of rebellion and submission.[18]

[17] Sigmund Freud, "Some Character-Types Met With in Psycho-analytic Work," in his *Collected Papers* (New York: Basic Books, Inc., 1959), IV, 318–344. See also Nietzsche's earlier depiction of this type in "On the Pale Criminal" in his *Thus Spoke Zarathustra* or Dostoevsky's perfect embodiment of it in the character of Raskolnikov in *Crime and Punishment.*

[18] This same balance, this same tolerance of ambiguity or disparity, is fundamental to democratic governance at large. See Harry Eckstein, "A Theory of Stable Democracy," Princeton University Center of International Studies Monograph #2, 1961.

Churchill's comparison of Saint George's and the reformatories further stands as an accusation of Sneyd-Kynnersley (and, we might surmise, his father as well) for his cruelty, and an affirmation of Churchill's own benevolence as a political leader. He is saying that he treated his children, his recalcitrant schoolboys—that is, the English people—far better than did his father or his headmaster. Finally, he is also acknowledging his identification with the figures of authority from his childhood; he is proclaiming his own power and right to be a political father, a political headmaster.

We will return to what is, in fact, Churchill's striking identification with his father in the next section. Here we should note that the stark brutality of Churchill's first school experiences was moderated after he left Saint George's. A school in Brighton, run by two gentle old ladies, and Harrow were relatively humane, and at least did nothing to intensify Winston's feelings of hostility. But his persistent academic laziness and pranks culminated in his father's decision that Winston should be prepared for a military career: Lord Randolph thought his son lacked sufficient intelligence to be a barrister! [19]

It cannot be said that Winston was distressed at the prospect of a military life. He was fascinated by soldiery and war, so fascinated that he had acquired a huge collection of toy soldiers, with which he continued to play well into adolescence. With his cooperative troops, he could release the pent-up hostilities of school and family life, playing the role of English general and administering beatings to the opposing forces. In this way he was able to compensate for the emotional beatings he continued to receive from his father and his teachers. [20]

Much of Churchill's happiness during his school days (that is, during the later part of latency and early adolescence) came from the realm of phantasy. His dreams of military glory were expressed with his toy soldiers, his dreams of political achievement fed on his father's spectacular political career, [21] and his relationship to his parents was largely fictional. Or, to put the last point another way,

[19] Winston Churchill, *My Early Life,* p. 19.

[20] In technical terms, one would say that Churchill was turning passivity into activity: he was doing to others something that had been done to him. Freud's original statement of the idea is in *Beyond the Pleasure Principle* (*Standard Ed.,* 18).

[21] Between 1880 and 1886 Lord Randolph rose from the position of Tory backbencher to Chancellor of the Exchequer and Leader of the Conservatives in the House of Commons. His stay at the top was, however, short-lived, so that Winston, during his adolescence, was witness to the political and physical decline of his father.

Churchill's contact with his parents was so minimal that he had to create out of his own imagination a loving relationship with them. Once he entered school, he was visited only rarely by either parent, often had to spend his vacations at school to make up for his negligence during the term, and, when he was given a holiday, was seldom permitted to spend it with Lord and Lady Randolph. His contact with them, especially his mother, was almost entirely by mail. Letters from his mother became his emotional lifeline, his one precarious link to the most important people in his life. Out of these letters and his own imagination he had to create a picture of a loving mother and father.

Two of the consequences of the role of phantasy in Churchill's late childhood are that he did not seek deep emotional ties outside his family and that he developed the skills appropriate to his daydreams. Emotionally, he was almost exclusively involved with family matters. He formed few friendships at school, and was considered to be something of a snob. In later life, political power and his motherland replaced his parents as important emotional objects. Concrete human beings always occupied a position of secondary significance.

Churchill was not content, however, simply to dream of great victories or the love of his mother. He also worked hard to build the skills that each enterprise demanded. He carefully studied great British battles, trying to understand the tactics and strategy that culminated in victory. So well, in fact, did he learn his lessons that he was exceptionally well prepared for Sandhurst Military Academy in these respects. He also rode assiduously and gained considerable skill in the use of side arms. And, more importantly in the long run, he learned to speak and write the English language with grace and accuracy. Well-written letters were, after all, virtually his only means of appealing to his mother.[22] In sum, both the penchant for emotional independence and the skills he was to exploit militarily and politically existed in at least nascent form as Churchill approached adolescence.

Adolescence and Young Manhood

As has been mentioned, Winston and his father agreed that a military career would be best for him. Hence in 1889, when he was fifteen, Winston was placed in the so-called Army Class at Harrow. This curriculum was designed to allow any reasonably bright young man to pass the wide-ranging but rather shallow examinations that

---

[22] The fact that he was considered to be too stupid to work extensively with foreign languages and was therefore given repeated exposure to the fundamentals of English grammar was undoubtedly a help in this regard.

qualified one for admission to Sandhurst. Winston, however, continued his habitual negligence in these courses as in his others, and consequently failed the examinations the first two times he took them. It is against this background that we must see the following important episode.

Winston was home for a brief vacation before resuming preparations for another (and finally successful) attempt to pass the examinations. He was playing a variant of hide-and-seek with his brother and a cousin when he found himself trapped on a bridge over a gulley. With his brother approaching from one side and his cousin from the other, capture seemed certain. The only alternative, a risky one, was to jump off the bridge, slide down one of the tall pine trees adjacent to it, and safely reach the ground. He decided to take the risk:

In a second I had plunged, throwing out my arms to embrace the summit of the fir tree. The argument [that such an escape was possible] was correct; the data were absolutely wrong. It was three days before I regained consciousness and more than three months before I crawled from my bed.[23]

Although he exaggerates somewhat the length of his convalescence, Winston's injuries were severe. One might think, therefore, that the experience would have a sobering effect on the reckless and careless young man, that henceforth he would be more prudent. The result was, however, quite the opposite; Winston's unwillingness to surrender and his boldness in the face of danger were even more pronounced in the years to come.

What factors are involved in this perhaps surprising outcome? Most simply, Winston suffered no permanent ill effects from the exploit. Just as he had survived the fall from the donkey in Ireland, so he survived his plunge from the bridge. His sense of personal invulnerability was thus not damaged; indeed, such close encounters with death gave him a sense of destiny, a faith in a personal star that was preserving him for great deeds. In the years to come, Churchill was to be in danger, militarily or politically, with startling frequency. He was always taking the big risk, the leap from the bridge; and he usually landed on his feet. It is not wonder, then, that he slept easily the night he became Prime Minister.

Here we may pause to note that Churchill's sensitivity to aggression during his early childhood, his recalcitrance at school, his leap from the bridge, and his incessant courting of military and political

[23] Winston Churchill, *My Early Life,* pp. 29–30.

danger after he left school all bear witness to his feelings of guilt
for his own hostile impulses. The relatively minor injuries or "punishment" he absorbed as a consequence served both to gratify his
conscience and to reassure him that he could survive even the punishment he inflicted, or caused to be inflicted, upon himself.

Churchill not only survived the plunge from the bridge, he was, in
a most important way, rewarded for it; for the first time, both
parents really paid attention to him. They brought in the best Harley
Street physicians, canceled their other plans, and, when he was con-
valescent, allowed him to participate in family affairs. He even
visited the House of Commons as his father's guest and was permitted to converse with his father's friends. In short, the reward for
his daring plunge was some semblance of the love and respect he had
so long craved. Thus when he was later confronted by situations involving grave risks, he might, unconsciously, have expected similar
results from taking them.

Had this more favorable relationship with his parents continued
over the next several years, it is possible that Churchill's career might
have been rather different; but, despite the young man's undying
hopes, his parents soon relapsed into their habitual disinterest and,
on the part of his father, hostility. At this time (1893–1895) Lord
Randolph was a sick man, physically and, increasingly, mentally.
Occasionally considerate of his son, as in the bridge incident, he was
more often harsh and condemning. Yet Winston absorbed his father's
abuse with little protest and virtually no indignation. It is thus fair
to surmise that the ambivalence that underlay Winston's attitude
toward his father became, if anything, more intense at this time. This
ambivalence is well captured in Churchill's description of his relationship to his father prior to Lord Randolph's death in January, 1895:

In fact to me he seemed to own the key to everything or almost everything
worth having. But if ever I began to show the slightest idea of comrade-
ship, he was immediately offended; and when once I suggested that I
might help his private secretary to write some of his letters, he froze me
into stone. I know now that this would have been only a passing phase.
Had he lived another four or five years, he could not have done without
me.[24]

On the one hand, Lord Randolph rejected Winston almost totally;
on the other, he could not do without his son in the long run. Here
we see vividly presented the internal war between reality and day-

[24] *Ibid.,* p. 46.

dream, between the fact of antagonistic familial relations and the wish for closeness and love.

Churchill's ambivalence toward his father had, moreover, implications for his career. Should he become a soldier, as his father wished him to do, and as he was not a little inclined to do himself? Or should he try to win his father's approval for a political career, approval his father was most unwilling to give. In the month's before his father's death, these questions, latently or manifestly, must have posed themselves to Churchill, who was busy giving his first public addresses while successfully concluding his stay at Sandhurst. Lord Randolph's death meant, however, that Churchill could not receive his father's help, approval, or rejection. Any of these alternatives would have made the task of choosing a career, a professional identity, easier; instead, Churchill had to create out of his own psychological resources a solution to the problem.

The task of choosing a career was not only not simplified by Lord Randolph's death, it was substantially complicated; for, given Winston's unconscious hostility for his father and the reproaches the elder man had heaped upon him, it is not too much to suppose that his feelings of guilt would have been heightened by Lord Randolph's death. Yet even this added psychic burden did not cause Winston to attempt an "escape from freedom," to use Erich Fromm's phrase, an escape from ambivalence by becoming either a dutiful soldier or a rebel of some kind. Now, as earlier, he did not elect the extremes; he chose rather to continue living with ambiguity and stress. This course of action was made tolerable by, first, combining the military and political sides of his personality into one professional identity and, second, by an intensified identification with his father.

We have already seen that Churchill's martial activities provided him with an outlet for his feelings of hostility for his father while giving him a sense of his father's approval. His inclination toward politics, by contrast, expressed his need to compete with his father more directly, to enter the lists with him for the prize of England's esteem. The fact that his father was dead meant only that the competition took place within Churchill's personality, that it became increasingly an intrapsychic conflict.

By using his military activities to serve his political ends, and by treating politics as a form of military campaigning, Churchill was able to create a precarious balance among the conflicting emotions that underlay his personality. The balance frequently broke down, leaving Churchill deeply depressed; but on the whole he could offset, say, the guilt accruing to political activity by risking his life in military activity, or the feeling of subservience of army life by breaking army rules in the interest of political advancement. This pattern remained essentially unchanged even after Churchill left the army in 1899.

The balance Churchill managed to achieve between these sides of his personality would hardly have been possible if he had felt that political action was a direct challenge to his father, or his father's memory: the burden of guilt would have been far too heavy. But one consequence of the loss of someone we love, especially someone whom we love ambivalently, is a tendency to identify with the lost person, to internalize his characteristics.[25] In this way we manage to keep at least some trace of the person alive. Churchill, it seems clear, identified himself with his father after the latter's death. Manifestly he thought of himself as his father's heir. His first speeches in the House of Commons, to which he was elected in 1900, were on his father's pet issues and evoked his father's positions. He sought out his father's friends and tried to keep alive his political legacy. By these actions, we might surmise, Churchill sought to placate his conscience, to show his father how loyal he was.

His identification with Lord Randolph did not end in the espousal of his views. He also started to walk like his father, talk like his father, finger his lapel as his father had, dress as his father had dressed, and sit where, and in the same slouched position in which, his father had sat in the House. At first this mimicry attracted satirical attention, but it eventually became so much Churchill's natural way of doing things that others accepted it as natural too. Thus one might say that Churchill managed to transform himself, psychologically, into his father without, however, merely being a carbon copy. And because he identified so strongly with his personal model of supreme power and authority, he was usually confident of his strength and his right. And England, during the time Churchill termed her "finest hour," shared that confidence, and gave him the love and respect he had so long craved.

Political Man

Let us see if we can use Churchill's life experiences to provide a basis for a psychological model of, first, political men in general and, second, political leaders in particular.

If Churchill is a fair example, then for political men, as indeed for

[25] See Freud's treatment of this subject in "Mourning and Melancholia," *Collected Papers*, IV, 152–170.

all men, there is a continuity of style and motivation from the experiences of childhood to those of adult life. Churchill's continuing involvement with his father and later substitutes for his father, his
early and pervasive sensitivity to aggression, especially in military
form are just two examples from among many. Political activity, to
add a second point, appears to gratify basic emotional needs: political men use public affairs to control and express their feelings,
as well as to exercise skills. Thus we saw Churchill achieving a tolerable relationship with his father's memory and gaining, in surrogate form, his mother's love through his political endeavors. The
word "surrogate," in turn, tells us that the bridge from the sphere
of private motives to that of public action is the displacement of
emotion, the substitution of public for private objects. In this regard, the feelings and longings Churchill had for his mother were
transferred onto the English nation; the ambivalence about his father,
onto other male authorities, enemies of the English nation and—in a
most crucial way—onto himself. Finally, some kind of political creed
is developed or accepted as a guide to, and rationalization for, political action. With Churchill this process did not go much beyond
the enunciation of the credo cited on page 17, and *ad hoc* pro-
nouncements in reaction to changing circumstances.

This set of generalizations about political men was first put forward
by Harold D. Lasswell in his ground breaking *Psychopathology and
Politics*, first published in 1930. In that work he provided a concise
expression of these points, one which has guided all subsequent work
in the field of psychoanalysis and politics:

$$p\}d\}r = P$$

or, *private motives displaced onto public objects and rationalized in
terms of the public interest result in political man.*[26]

In later works, Lasswell has elaborated this formulation somewhat further. In *Power and Personality*, for example, he argues that
political men expect the wielding of power to help them overcome low
estimates of self (meaning by "self" both themselves as individuals
and the group for which they claim to speak or act). Presumably
their self-esteem has been damaged somewhere along the path to
maturity, and as adults they attempt to compensate for this damage
by gaining deference through political means. As a result, the focus
of their emotional lives shifts from the private to the public spheres
by the combined use of displacement and rationalization. Through

[26] See Lasswell's *Psychopathology and Politics* (New York: The Viking
Press, 1960), p. 262.

displacement, public objects, such as the state, empire, church, or
working class, are substituted for private ones; and, through rationalization (the acceptance or development of a belief system about
the public sphere), political activity is justified.[27]

With sufficient investigative resources, it could probably be dem-
onstrated that Lasswell's formulation holds quite generally for men
who devote their lives to political activity.[28] Our analysis of Churchill
is, for example, congruent with Lasswell's model, and we shall see
that Malcolm X and Nietzsche are also at least partially explicable
in these terms. We should not, however, confuse a plausible partial
explanation with a fully tested inclusive one. Without genuinely
systematic testing, no more than plausibility can be claimed for
the ideas we are using here. Political men, moreover, grow out of
much more complex conditions than our general formulation might
seem to imply. For Churchill a wide range of situational factors, such
as his family's prominent position in English society and a degree of
fluidity in party politics which permitted him to follow his own distinctive course of action, were necessary concomitants of political
success. Even psychologically, in fact, the evolution of Churchill's
political personality and its operation are not explicable entirely
through the formula of compensation through displacement and
rationalization. Churchill was not only compensating for low self-
esteem, but also seeking objects to love and objects to hate; he repressed his aggressive feelings toward his father and projected those
feelings onto other authorities, as well as using displacement as such;
and his use of rationalizations was simple and unchanging in a general
sense while being highly flexible in particular instances.

We must not, in other words, expect general formulations to substitute for detailed analysis. As a starting point, however, Lasswell's
formulation is extremely useful and can fruitfully serve as the basis
for more detailed explorations.

Political Leaders

Political leaders are, of course, political men; accordingly, we
understand their behavior partly in terms of the ideas outlined in
the preceding section. In this same way, it might be mentioned,
political men are just one variety of the species man, and therefore
are explained partly in terms of our conception of human nature.

---

[27] This elaboration is derived from Lasswell's *Power and Personality* (New
York: The Viking Press, 1962), pp. 37–41.

[28] See the bibliography for some of the major works in this area.

Leaders like Churchill have in addition, however, that set of char-acteristics alluded to in the first part of this chapter. There it was argued that leaders crave, relish, and have confidence in their own power and authority. Now it may be hypothesized that these char-acteristics result from, in large part, the leader's relationship to his father. His father is his first model of power and authority, strength and rectitude, a model he seeks to emulate. At the same time, his feelings for his father are ambivalent; he both loves and hates his father, and expects the latter to reciprocate.

What his been described is, of course, nothing other than the normal oedipal configuration. What appears to be crucial for the leader is its intensity and duration. We saw, for example, that Churchill was, throughout his childhood, deprived of the contact that would have humanized his father and made it easier for the son to outgrow him. This intensification by distance was then joined to Lord Randolph's premature death, so that Churchill was de-prived of the possibility of testing his young manhood against a living model and competitor. The result was the prolongation of his concern with questions of domination and rights on the one hand, and his identification with his father on the other. The former con-sequence underlay his interest in politics; the latter, his ability to play the leader's role.

The leader's extraordinary identification with the father's role, coupled with the displacement of that role to the political sphere, is his most distinguishing attribute. It also helps to explain the linked feelings of aloneness and superiority to which leaders are prone. For the father is, within the family, the supreme arbiter, the final judge. None can fully share his responsibilities of his prerogatives. He ap-pears to his young children, moreover, to be a creature of almost in-describable majesty. No normal human being could compete with the image he implants in his children's minds were it not for the possibility of growing up while he grows old. The political leader seems to be, either physically or emotionally, denied this experience. He thus identifies not simply with a man, but with a demigod.

This identification is never quite complete. In fact, if it were, we would have a man who consciously thought of himself as his father, or as God the Father. Leaders, by contrast, seldom confuse them-selves with God. Rather, they often think of themselves as God's servant, as his favorite son, just as Churchill thought of himself as his father's political heir. But they are fiercely loyal to, and fully under the sway of, their God, their father, and they can tolerate no other man on earth as a full replacement.

It should be mentioned that, under unusual circumstances, an identification with the mother may substitute for an identification with the father. Mohandas Gandhi's political personality, and the nonviolent techniques it involved, were largely derived from his mother's characteristics and ways of exerting influence in the family.[29] Such men invert the normal oedipal relationship: they seek the father's love the way most boys seek the mother's. Churchill, and most political leaders, display rather an accentuation of the normal oedipal configuration: they identify intensely with their fathers in the attempt to gain the mother's love; they play devotedly the role of political father to gain the love of the motherland.

The intense and unresolvable oedipal relationship also helps to account for the leader's single-mindedness. The leader appears to be a man whose conflicts throughout life circle narrowly around the same emotional center. Thus we saw that Churchill's feelings and interests seldom strayed very far from, metaphorically speaking, Horatius at the bridge.

The leader's single-mindedness is connected in turn with his ability to sever relationships with even his most intimate associates when this becomes necessary. For the leader invests virtually all his emotional energy in the role and ends that enable him to manage the ambivalences and contradictions of his personality. Thus other people do not fully exist for him emotionally. In Churchill's case, the lack of intimacy in his childhood resulted in his carrying this tendency to unusual lengths, to the point where he was often insensitive to the demands being placed upon him by his followers and the British public at large. Other leaders manage to strike a more effective balance between emotional involvement and withdrawal, one that allows them to perceive the feelings of others while continuing to treat them instrumentally. This characteristic, repugnant as it might be to our moral sensibilities, is an attribute of democratic as well as nondemocratic leaders. Hence any system of political morality which does not deal with it is sure to be incomplete and of limited utility.

A final characteristic of leaders which is largely determined by their relationships to their fathers is their proclivity to seek out, and ability to manage, conflict. In the first place, aggression is motivationally very important for these men. Much of Churchill's career, for example, can be viewed as a way of finding suitable objects against whom to release the hostility built up toward his father. But while Churchill was deeply involved in aggressive activity, he was not a

---

[29] I examine the relationship between Gandhi's identification with his mother and his political style in *The Revolutionary Personality* (Princeton: Princeton University Press, 1967).

specialist in violence. A leader like Hitler who was, by contrast, obsessed by violence is more the exception than the rule, just as Gandhi is at the other extreme. Most political leaders seem to be more capable of tolerating ambivalence, and gain more satisfaction from so doing, than either the destroyer or the saint. They have learned to deal successfully with their own internal conflicts short of the annihilation of either 'their loving or aggressive capacities; and they seek, consciously or unconsciously, to apply these same basic techniques to politics. When these men must resort to force, or feel inclined to do so, they find it necessary to provide elaborate justifications of their actions. Such rationalizations, we would guess, serve to placate their consciences as well as their constituencies.

The simplest summary of what has been contended so far is that political leaders manage conflict within their personalities, especially ambivalent feelings for their fathers, by playing the role of father in the public sphere. As was mentioned above, the techniques by which they do this tend to become the basis of their political style; and the problems they manage to resolve become their models of the fundamental issues of politics. Churchill's basic dilemma, the dilemma of loyalty to or rebellion against his father, was resolved by his linking together political and military vocations. This linkage, his militancy in politics and his political astuteness in military matters, then became the distinguishing characteristic of his political style. He attempted to transform, moreover, as many situations as possible into political-military ones—thus the fiasco at Sidney Street, and thus his successful efforts to ready the British fleet before World War I.

There is a further sense in which the management of internal conflict serves as the model for the management of conflict in general. Displacement, for example, was one of the defenses Churchill used to lower the intensity of his feelings of guilt. He worked out his feelings of aggression for his father with his teachers, toy soldiers, and other father surrogates. He also used this technique in a manifestly political way. When, early in his career, he could not gain the favors he needed from one public official, he would shift to another; when frustrated in achieving his goals politically, he would return temporarily to the military. As First Lord of the Admiralty during World War I, he was blamed for the disaster of the Dardanelles campaign. Forced to resign his cabinet post, he rejoined the Army and went to the Front to fight.

In other words, there is a correlation between such things as intrapsychic flexibility and tactical flexibility in politics. The man who uses a rigid pattern of defense to control his own impulses, who cannot take advantage of the nonpathological possibilities for displacement and rationalization early in his life and in the private sphere generally, is not likely to operate effectively in political situations calling for subtlety and the ability to adjust to changing conditions.[30]

The above points intimate that some leaders are more or less rigid, more or less realistic, more or less militant than others. Let us, in the remainder of the chapter, take a look at some of the variations among political leaders.

Varieties of Political Leaders

There are numerous ways of subdividing the general category of leaders into more specific groupings. We can think of totalitarian leaders, democratic leaders, and traditional authoritarian leaders; revolutionary and reactionary leaders; western and nonwestern leaders; and so on almost indefinitely. The selection of any one such range of variation over any other is, to some extent, arbitrary; but questions of the roles leaders play, their attitude toward political change, and their propensity to use or abjure violent means are clearly worth raising.

The major work on correlations between personality types and political roles is again Harold Lasswell's. In the works already cited, Lasswell studied men who performed well or poorly in a broad range of political positions. Out of this work he concluded that two major personality types, the *compulsive* character and the *dramatizing* character, appear with great frequency in politics—the compulsive (but not neurotically compulsive) person as an effective administrator; the dramatizer as an effective agitator.[31]

The compulsive character is "distinguished by the degree to which it relies upon rigid, obsessive ways of handling human relations," while the dramatizer demands an "immediate affective response from others."[32] Lasswell then argues that the more compulsive type selects limited and relatively stereotyped goals for political achievement, seeks orderly procedures for reaching such goals, treats people as objects to be manipulated rather than as human beings with feelings,

[30] One cannot but be struck by the applicability of the vocabulary of psychodynamics to such varied phenomena as political tactics, family life, aesthetic and philosophical technique, dreams, mental disturbance, wit and humor. In, for example, the centrality of repression (using the concept in a nonspecific sense) to virtually all areas of life, there are intimations of understanding which have yet to be fully realized.

[31] See *Psychopathology and Politics,* Chaps. VI–VIII *passim.,* and *Personality and Politics,* Chap. IV.

[32] Lasswell, *Personality and Politics,* p. 62.

avoids situations involving many "unknowns," and presents himself to others as blandly as possible.

In relatively pure form, the compulsive is more likely to be found in a bureaucratic post than at the head of a political organization or movement. But a substantial tendency toward compulsion was a part of the leadership style of men as diverse as Lenin, Gandhi, and Woodrow Wilson.[33] Each of these men was an effective administrator; each sought the orderliness and control that the type implies. Yet each of these men had many of the characteristics of the dramatizer as well. They chose for themselves ambitious and unorthodox goals, dealt with the unknowns of innovative politics, were often sensitive to the responses of others, and enjoyed drawing attention to themselves, enjoyed the response of an audience.[34] Effective leaders have, in other words, as one of their major attributes the ability to incorporate into one personality pattern elements that would be incompatible for most men.

The three men mentioned above had a common commitment to social and political change, although they differed on goals and means. Any leader, in fact, can be ranked along a scale of commitment to change, such as that developed by A. Lawrence Lowell: [35]

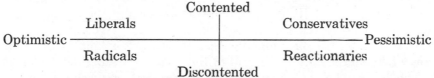

Lowell thus ranks men in terms of their optimism about the future on the one hand, and their contentment or lack of contentment with things in the present on the other. By this scheme Churchill is a conservative; Wilson, a liberal; Lenin, a radical; and Hitler, a reactionary.

A second way of looking at attitudes toward change is that developed by Erik H. Erikson in *Young Man Luther.* There he argues that men, especially young men, commit themselves to change in order to effect changes in themselves, in order to resolve their personal crises of identity:

In some young people, in some classes, at some periods in history, [the identity] crisis will be minimal; in other people, classes, and periods, the crisis will be clearly marked off as a critical period, a kind of "second

[33] On Woodrow Wilson, see Alexander and Juliette George, *Woodrow Wilson and Colonel House* (New York: The John Day Co., 1956); on Lenin and Gandhi, see *The Revolutionary Personality.*

[34] Lenin was somewhat less "dramatic" in these ways than the other two men.

[35] Cited in Lasswell, *Power and Personality,* p. 60.

birth," apt to be aggravated either by widespread neuroticisms or by pervasive ideological unrest. Some young individuals will succomb to this
crisis in all manner of neurotic, psychotic and delinquent behavior; others
will resolve it through participation in ideological movements passionately
concerned with religion or politics, nature or art. Still others, although
suffering and deviating dangerously through what appears to be a prolonged adolescence, eventually come to contribute an original bit to an
emerging style of life; the very danger which they have sensed has forced
them to mobilize capacities to see and say, to dream and plan, to design
and construct, in new ways.[36]

Erikson's statement, like Lowell's schema, is highly general. Together,
however, they constitute a starting point for the study of attitudes
toward change.[37]

Before turning to a brief consideration of the propensity toward
violence in politics, let us note that the most dramatic class of political innovators, the revolutionists, rely very heavily on a particular
way of dealing with the ambivalence of the father-son relationship.
For the revolutionist, it is both possible and necessary to split that
ambivalence neatly into positive and negative components when displacing it to the political sphere. Although Churchill was most effective politically when he had a foreign enemy, like Hitler, to fight, he
remained ambivalently loyal to both his father and the political system his father served throughout his life. Lenin, by contrast, found
in the memory of Marx and the idea of History a kind of paternal
deity he could loyally serve, and in the Tsar a paternal devil against
which he could fight. This splitting of ambivalence was, of course,
facilitated by the conditions of Russian life at the time; but Lenin's
relationship to his father was a necessary condition of his revolutionary world view.[38]

Occasionally one finds in politics a man who abjures the use of violence altogether, as did Gandhi; or, unfortunately not quite as rarely,
men like Hitler for whom violence is a matter of policy. Most leaders,
like Lenin and Churchill, fall somewhere between these poles. Where
they fall seems to depend upon three basic psychological conditions,
which may be stated in the following hypothetical form: (1) the
lower the level of active guilt, the greater the propensity to use violent
means; (2) the greater the perceived dangerousness and animosity of

[36] Erik H. Erikson, *Young Man Luther* (New York: W. W. Norton and
Company, Inc., 1958), pp. 14–15.

[37] Erikson does in fact develop these points further in *Young Man Luther*
and subsequent contributions.

[38] For a more detailed consideration, see *The Revolutionary Personality*,
Chaps. 2 and 3.

the enemy, the greater the propensity to use violent means; and (3) the higher the degree of masculine identification, the greater the propensity to use violent means.[39] The last of these hypotheses, as was implied earlier, states the correlation, in someone like Gandhi, between his identification with his mother and his reliance on nonviolence. Men like Churchill, who identify very strongly with their fathers, are less reticent about the use of force.

The second hypothesis is more or less self-evident: a man like Churchill, who saw Nazi Germany as a threat to his country, reacts more willingly with preparations for war than one like Neville Chamberlain, who persisted in seeing Hitler as nothing more than a rather militant German nationalist until it was almost too late to react. The origins of such a perception are, of course, not so simple. Churchill's image of Hitler was derived in part from his picture of his father, as well as from a realistic idea of Hitler's intentions.

The first point is perhaps less obvious. We saw in Churchill's case that guilt is a very complicated feeling, that it can lead as easily to criminality as to dutiful submission. When it is actively and consciously felt as guilt, rather than repressed and projected, it serves as a strong check on violence. When it is denied and kept from consciousness, it is perhaps the most powerful impetus to violence.

Questions of criminality and dutiful obedience, of violence and love, are basic not only to the study of political leaders, but also to our understanding of political adherents. Malcolm X, to whom we now turn, was involved in this web of feeling, this set of choices, no less than Churchill.

[39] These points are taken from E. Victor Wolfenstein, "Violence or Non-Violence: A Psychoanalytic Exploration of the Choice of Political Means in Social Change," Princeton University Center of International Studies Monograph #20, 1965.

3

Political Adherents

Political leaders and adherents share several manifest qualities. Both are fundamentally concerned with matters of power and authority, single-mindedly devoted to the realization of their political goals, and experts in the uses of conflict. But adherents, unlike leaders, think of themselves as being subordinate to at least one other man, as Malcolm X was to Elijah Muhammad. Although they may be leaders themselves, they do so in the name and under the direction of another man. Thus Malcolm X commanded the loyalty of a great many of his fellow black men, and the respect of not a few white men; but it was not until the last months of his tragically short life that he attempted to lead in his own right. By studying the genesis and character of Malcolm's relationship to Elijah Muhammad, therefore, we may expect to gain some understanding of the psychology of adherency.

Malcolm X as Political Adherent: "We Have a Common Enemy" [1]

Malcolm X sought, for himself and his fellow black men, power that was not dependent upon the beneficence of white men, and a sense of rectitude that was not dependent upon their God. Similarly Churchill had fought to maintain Britain's power as a nation, never doubting her right to her national or imperial status.[2] Both men, in addition, utilized political organizations in working for their personal and col-

[1] Malcolm X, "Message to the Grass Roots," in George Breitman, ed., *Malcolm X Speaks* (New York: Grove Press, 1966), p. 5.

[2] Malcolm was, of course, seeking to create power and authority for his people, Churchill, to preserve it.

40

lective goals. Malcolm X, for most of his career, dedicated himself to the Nation of Islam (the so-called Black Muslims), through which he hoped to alter radically the position of black men in American life. Churchill served and was served by both the Liberal and Conservative parties during his political career.

Yet Churchill, unlike Malcolm X, looked forward eagerly to the time when he would lead his nation; and he was willing to risk friendships and change party affiliations in the process. Malcolm X thought of himself not as a leader, but as the loyal follower of Elijah Muhammad, the Prophet and Messenger of Allah:

> My adoration of Mr. Muhammad grew, in the sense of the Latin root word *adorare*. It means much more than our "adoration" or "adore." It means that my worship of him was so awesome that he was the first man whom I had ever feared—not fear such as of a man with a gun, but the fear such as one has of the power of the sun.[3]

Or, as Malcolm put it many times in his public speeches:

> I have sat at our Messenger's feet, hearing the truth from his own mouth! I have pledged on my knees to Allah to tell the white man about his crimes and the black man the true teachings of our Honorable Elijah Muhammad. I don't care if it costs my life. . . .[4]

Churchill was a leader, a man who served no other living human being; Malcolm X was a disciple, a proselytizer of a religious and political faith.

Malcolm X was as single-minded in his devotion to the leader and the organization he believed truly expressed the aspirations of his people as was Churchill in his loyalty to the English nation and its political system. Malcolm (whose surname at birth was Little) was converted to a belief in Islam while in prison. Shortly after his release in 1952, he joined the Nation as a full member and was renamed Malcolm X—the "X" signifying that he no longer was a captive of his "slave" identity. He quickly impressed Elijah Muhammad with his vigor and loyalty, was made assistant minister of the Detroit mosque, and was soon given responsibility for developing temples in such places as Boston, New York, Philadelphia, and Los Angeles. In each instance his oratory, organizational skills, and inventiveness gained him notable success. It was Malcolm X, for example, who was most responsible for developing new and more effective ways of financ-

---

[3] Malcolm X, *The Autobiography of Malcolm X* (New York: Grove Press, 1966), p. 212.
[4] *Ibid.*, p. 210.

ing the Nation's activities; and it was Malcolm who originated *Mr. Muhammad Speaks*, the movement's major newspaper and publicity organ.[5] One might summarize Malcolm's contribution to the Nation of Islam by noting that when he joined it was not very different from many of the other cults that have traditionally been popular among urban Negroes. It was little known and had under a thousand members.[6] When Elijah Muhammad forced him out of the movement in 1964, it was one of the most powerful and feared organizations of black men in the country. And, as Churchill had been the English lion's roar during World War II, so Malcolm had been the angry, articulate voice of the Muslims. After his departure, Elijah Muhammad's message was not as easily heard or as well received.

During the twelve years he was a follower of Elijah Muhammad, Malcolm gave almost all of his eighteen waking hours a day to the movement. He regulated his life carefully by the wristwatch from which he was never parted. He traveled untiringly from one end of the country to the other organizing, exhorting, challenging, and guiding his people; confronting, debating, shocking and disturbing the "enemy," the "Man," the "white devil." He found time to marry a Muslim sister and raise a family; but his suitcase and briefcase were always packed, he was often away from home for weeks at a time, and, when he was home, he was almost always preoccupied with Muslim affairs.

Malcolm was distinctive among the followers of Elijah Muhammad not only for his energy, devotion, and articulate speech, but also for his desire to direct the movement into the political arena, to bring to a head the seething conflict between black and white in America. Thus in 1959, when the police arrested a Muslim brother in Harlem, Malcolm led a group of about fifty members of the Fruit of Islam (the elite guard of the movement) to the police station where the man was being held. He gained access to the prisoner, who was in need of medical attention, and secured hospital care for him. The consequence was that, as Malcolm put it, "for the first time the black man, woman, and child in the streets was discussing 'those Muslims.' " [7] After this incident, Malcolm became more outspoken than ever before on political matters and pressed Elijah Muhammad to commit the brotherhood to political combat.

---

[5] *Ibid.*, pp. 211–265 *passim*. Also see C. Eric Lincoln, *The Black Muslims in America* (Boston: Beacon Press, 1961).

[6] Malcolm himself estimates that the movement had about four hundred members when he joined (*The Autobiography.* . . . p. 410).

[7] *Ibid.*, p. 235.

Malcolm's increasing emphasis on politics, as well as Elijah Muhammad's fear of Malcolm's following within the movement, led to his separation from the Nation in 1964. Unlike Churchill, who crossed party lines about as easily as walking across a street, Malcolm was profoundly disturbed by the break with the man he had worshipped and the brotherhood he had helped to build: "My head felt like it was bleeding inside. I felt like my brain was damaged." [8] For more than a decade Malcolm had been a follower of a prophet, an apostle of a creed, a member of a religious family. He had been Malcolm X, the angriest Muslim. Now he was alone, once more an individual. He soon discovered, moreover, that Elijah Muhammad was not prepared to tolerate his apostasy, that orders had been given to kill him. Pursued by many of his former brothers, by the same Fruit of Islam he had helped to train, uncertain in his religious faith, and groping to define his political goals, Malcolm appealed from the Prophet to Allah: he decided to make the pilgrimage to Mecca.

The result of Malcolm's journey to the holy city of Islam was a broadening of his conception of the Moslem faith, a weakening of his unequivocal rejection of all things white, and a desire to link the causes of American black men and oppressed peoples around the world. This new outlook was expressed in the group he created upon his return, the Organization of Afro-American Unity (OAAU). And he adopted for himself a new name: El-Hajj Malik El-Shabazz.

Malcolm X was assassinated on February 21, 1965. The last months of his life, the months during which he was attempting to develop a program and a following for the OAAU, were overshadowed by the threat of imminent death. It is hence difficult to evaluate the short period when he tried to stand alone, when he tried to be a leader. It is apparent, however, that Malcolm was having difficulty gaining adherents, defining his political principles, and conveying to others an unambiguous picture of who he was. Was he an angry young man, a black nationalist, a believer in the brotherhood of man, a Moslem, or a man trying to ignore religious and racial distinctions? To many he appeared confused; to others, self-contradictory. The familiar passion was still there; but it was no longer—or, more likely, not yet—possible to tell what beliefs were to give it meaning, what faith was to give it direction.

We may thus view Malcolm's mature life as falling into three phases. First, there was a period of criminality culminating in a rather extended prison term. Second, Malcolm became a loyal adherent of

[8] *Ibid.*, p. 303.

Elijah Muhammad and the Muslim movement. Third, Malcolm left the Nation of Islam and tried to be a man in his own right. It is this pattern we will attempt to explain in the following section.

Initially, however, we may gain a more general perspective on Malcolm X in particular and adherents in general by utilizing Eric Hoffer's conception of the "true believer." [9]

The true believer is a man who is perpetually incomplete and insecure. He cannot generate self-assurance out of his individual resources—out of his rejected self—but finds it only by clinging passionately to whatever cause he happens to embrace.[10]

This statement nicely captures the apparently paradoxical character of men of intense belief. Malcolm X was, on the one hand, a man of great strength. His capacity for organizational work, his boldness and self-confidence when speaking, and his endless energy attest to this fact. On the other hand, it is also true that he gained his strength from his beliefs, his loyalties, and the role he was called upon to play. There is, in short, a symbiosis here: Malcolm X's work made the Muslims more powerful than ever before, and their power made it possible for Malcolm to do more and better work.

According to Hoffer, true believers are men with damaged souls, men needing a new self. They are often "sinners," men with a great sense of guilt, if not actual criminal records. The movement they join provides them with a way of sloughing off their sins, of redeeming themselves by loyal service to a leader or to God. In merging their individual identities into the collective identity of a mass movement, they gain the opportunity to start fresh, to do well what they have previously done poorly.

In the process of adopting a collective identity, such men tend to obliterate their individual selves. They define themselves in terms of the larger self of the brotherhood, as a part of a whole; and they partake thereby of the power and invulnerability of the larger unit. Malcolm Little, a criminal in prison, becomes Malcolm X, a part of the Nation of Islam.

The mass movements such men join also have a definite kind of ideology. This ideology devalues the present in favor of the future and the past. The damaged and aggressive actual self of the believer is attributed to the belittling and violent nature of the times; and he is assured that, at some future time, there will be universal peace and

[9] Eric Hoffer, *The True Believer* (New York: Mentor Books, 1951).
[10] *Ibid.,* p. 80.

tranquility. He may also be told that he is the descendent of a mighty people, has a glorious history, is part of a tradition of noble and heroic men, and so on. The true believer can thus say: It is only the present that is evil, or disappointing, or worthless; and because I transcend the present, because I exist in the past and future, I do not accept as real the present me, the existing me.[11]

What are the psychogenetic roots of Malcolm's career, of his alternating confused individuality and efficient adherency? What are the psychodynamic aspects of the adherent's personality? In the following section we will take up these questions; and briefly examine the psychological interaction of leader, ideology, and adherent in mass movements such as the Nation of Islam.

Malcolm X's Life

Early Childhood

Malcolm X begins his autobiography with the following incident:

> When my mother was pregnant with me, . . . a party of hooded Ku Klux Klan riders galloped up to our home. . . . Surrounding the house, brandishing their shotguns and rifles, they shouted for my father to come out. My mother went to the front door and opened it. Standing where they could see her pregnant condition, she told them that she was alone with her three small children, and that my father was away. . . . The Klansmen shouted threats and warnings at her that we had better get out of town because "the good Christian white people" were not going to stand for my father's "spreading trouble" among the "good" Negroes of Omaha with the "back to Africa" teachings of Marcus Garvey.[12]

Because his life was marked by racial violence and his own elaboration of a message similar to his father's, it is not surprising that Malcolm would use this event to set the tone for his narrative. The story has, however, a less obvious meaning as well. In his father's absence, it is his mother's pregnant condition that keeps the family from harm. Or, to view it another way, it is Malcolm himself, not yet born, who is the guardian, the defender of the family.

Such an interpretation may, at first glance, appear fanciful. Yet it is not too much to say that Malcolm's life was an attempt to realize this vision. He desired nothing more than to be his father's representative, his mother's defender, and his family's most loyal and coopera-

---

[11] *Ibid.,* pp. 66–78.
[12] Malcolm X, *The Autobiography . . . ,* p. 1.

tive member. These were the wishes that led him to become the voice and agent of Elijah Muhammad, the guarantor of the honor of Negro womanhood, and the major builder of the Nation of Islam.

Malcolm Little was born in Omaha, Nebraska, in 1925. His father, Earl Little, was a Baptist preacher and, as noted above, a follower of Marcus Garvey and his Universal Negro Improvement Association (UNIA). He was a big, strong, and very black man—qualities that, combined with his racial militancy, made him anathema to white supremacist groups wherever he went. To protect his family and escape persecution, he moved from Philadelphia to Omaha, from Omaha to Milwaukee, from Milwaukee to Lansing, Michigan. He married twice, the second time after the death of his first wife. Malcolm was the fourth of eight children resulting from the second marriage.

Malcolm, like his father, was tall and had a strong constitution; unlike Earl Little, he was very light skinned. This quality he inherited from his mother, Louise, a West Indian whose father was white. She "looked like a white woman," which made her especially attractive to her husband, and "her accent did not sound like a Negro's." [13] Her own strong beliefs, such as her dislike of pork and rabbit, which Earl Little relished, brought her into regular, and often physical, conflict with her husband.

The use of force was not confined to settling disputes between the parents:

My father was also belligerent toward all of the children, except me. The older ones he would beat almost savagely if they broke any of his rules—and he had so many rules it was hard to know them all. Nearly all of my whippings came from my mother. . . .[14]

Malcolm attributes his favored position with his father to his light skin color: "As anti-white as my father was, he was subconsciously so afflicted with the white man's brain-washing of Negroes that he inclined to favor the light [children], and I was his lightest child." [15]

The data cited thus far have several implications. First, we may note that Malcolm's relationship to his parents was quite different from Churchill's. Malcolm was his father's favorite and his mother's major disciplinary problem among the children; Churchill, although not close to either parent, received more affection from his mother

[13] *Ibid.,* p. 2
[14] *Ibid.,* p. 4.
[15] *Ibid.*

than from his father. Thus for Churchill the realities of his family situation would augment the oedipal tendency to identify with his father and seek his mother's love. For Malcolm, the relationship with his parents would produce, in addition, a tendency to identify with his mother and seek his father's love. Hence in later life Malcolm would search for *both* a mother and a father to love him, a search that culminated in his devotion to the light-skinned, gentle, and powerful Elijah Muhammad and to a creed notable for the multiplicity of its rules and the severity of its dietary regulations.

We may also discern, in Malcolm's description of his favored position with his father, signs of the ambivalence and guilt that were to lead him to accept eventually a new name and a new identity. He states that it was his light skin that won his father's esteem (and his mother's disfavor). But his father was attracted to light skin because he was "subconsciously so afflicted with the white man's brain-washing"; and his mother, from whom he inherited his color, was light because her father was a "white rapist." [16] Malcolm thus casts doubt on the sincerity of his father's affection for him (and on the reality of his mother's negative feelings). At the same time he is calling one male ancestor a rapist, and we may surmise that he is condemning his father, who was "belligerent" to his mother, by this appellation as well. In short, Malcolm may have doubted his father's love for him just because he doubted his own love for his father, and felt guilty for his unconscious aggressive impulses.

Churchill, we remember, similarly had ambivalent feelings for his father. He was able to manage these emotions by displacing all hostility, at least all manifest hostility, from himself and his family onto the surrounding environment. Malcolm, too, made use of displacement in managing his internal and familial conflicts. The clear antagonism of most white men to his father's militant teachings made such a shift rather easy. The intensity of his own antagonisms, however, and the manifest presence of conflict in the family made it impossible for him, on his own, either to live with or to split his ambivalent feelings. Rather an unhappy fusion of self-doubts and hostility was created, one that is well expressed in Malcolm's memory of an event that took place when he was about four years old:

I remember being suddenly snatched awake into a frightening confusion of pistol shots and shouting and smoke and flames. My father had shouted and shot at two white men who had set the fire and were running away. Our home was burning down around us. We were lunging and bumping

---

[16] *Ibid.*, p. 2.

and tumbling all over each other trying to escape. My mother, with the baby in her arms, just made it into the yard before the house crashed in showering sparks. I remember we were outside in the night in our underwear, crying and yelling our heads off. The white police and firemen came and stood around watching as the house burned to the ground.[17]

If we accept that this memory has, in addition to its manifest historical character, latent meaning as well, then we find in it a somber evocation of emotional confusion, of a self, a family, and a world pervaded by hostility and conflict, attack and defense. Earl Little, powerful though he may be, is not strong enough to stop the aggression of unfriendly white men. The members of the family, however much they love each other, are not able to remain calm and united in the face of attack. And, we will now see, Malcolm felt personally responsible for the catastrophies the family was soon to experience.

Despite the harassment that resulted from his activities, Malcolm's father continued his Garveyite preaching. He often took his favorite son with him, and Malcolm remembered being impressed by the quiet dignity of these gatherings in contrast to the jumping and shouting that was common at his father's Baptist services. He also remembered some of his father's phrases and slogans (such as "Up, you mighty race, you can accomplish what you will!"), and his emphasis on blackness and Africa. He had no clear conception of what was meant by this talk—he continued to think of Africa, for example, in terms of cannibals and tigers—but he certainly saw in it signs of his father's power and importance.

In his adult life, Malcolm was to identify himself with his father's role of militant preacher; but the possibility of a full and self-assured identification with his father, of the kind that Churchill possessed, was eliminated by Earl Little's death in 1931 when Malcolm was six.

On the day he died, Malcolm's father had been quarreling with his wife about the eating of rabbit, which she considered unclean. In anger, he had taken a rabbit from the pen:

He had pulled off the rabbit's head. He was so strong, he needed no knife to behead chickens or rabbits. With one twist of his big black hands he simply twisted off the head and threw the bleeding-necked thing at my mother's feet.[18]

Malcolm's mother, crying, started to skin the rabbit; and Malcolm, witnessing the scene, probably felt both terror and delight—terror

[17] *Ibid.*, p. 3.
[18] *Ibid.*, p. 9.

that his father's enormous power might be directed against him instead of the rabbit, delight in the strength he might one day hope to share.

Earl Little, his anger unappeased, left the house:

It was then that my mother had this vision. She . . . had always had a strong intuition of things about to happen. And most of her children are the same way, I think. When something is about to happen, I can feel something, sense something.[19]

For the rest of the day, Malcolm's mother was uneasy and nervous, afraid that something would happen to her husband. Malcolm, who identifies himself with his mother in the passage cited, may have shared her wordless dread. He also shared, one may suppose, his mother's sense of responsibility for what was to happen. For, as we shall also see when we turn to Nietzsche's life, the making of prophecies is usually a way of expressing a wish. Louise Little, consciously fearing something evil would befall her husband, unconsciously may have desired revenge for the humiliation and defeat she had just suffered. Malcolm, in choosing this place in his narrative to acknowledge his own prophetic intuition, is admitting his own unconscious desire for his father's demise.[20]

Malcolm was awakened in the middle of the night by the sound of his mother's screaming. She was taken to a hospital where her husband was dying:

My father's skull, on one side, was crushed in, I was told later. Negroes in Lansing have always whispered that he was attacked, and then laid across some tracks for a streetcar to run over him. His body was cut almost in half.[21]

Whether correctly or not, Malcolm came to blame the white man for his father's violent death, a death for which he unconsciously shared the guilt. At first, however, the idea of the white man's killing his father, like his father's racial pride, seems to have had little impact

[19] *Ibid.*

[20] Malcolm goes on to say, in reference to Elijah Muhammad:
   I have never known something to happen that has caught me completely off guard—except once. And that was when, years later, I discovered facts I couldn't believe about a man who, up until that discovery, I would gladly have given my life for.
By denying his prophetic powers when father figures are involved, Malcolm is trying to escape from his unconscious sense of responsibility for his father's fate.

[21] Malcolm X, *The Autobiography . . .*, p. 10.

on him. Indeed, his description of himself and his family gives us a feeling of shock and disbelief, of an inability to comprehend what has happened.

Malcolm remembers, the morning he learned of his father's death, a "vague commotion" in the house. His memory of the funeral is not "very clear" either; it "surprised" him that it was held in a funeral parlor instead of a church. A dreamlike aura thus surrounds Malcolm's description of the funeral:

[At the] service a big black fly came down and landed on my father's face, and Wilfred sprang up from his chair and he shooed the fly away, and he came groping back to his chair—there were folding chairs for us to sit on—and the tears were steaming down his face. When we went by the casket, I remember that I thought that it looked as if my father's strong black face had been dusted with flour, and I wished they hadn't put on such a lot of it.[22]

This passage, especially if read in context, has a faraway feeling absent from the rest of Malcolm's narrative. One senses in it a denial of the reality of the event, Malcolm's denial of his own feelings of loss and responsibility. It was not even a real funeral, for it was not held in a church!

This impression is strengthened by the way Malcolm describes his father's appearance in death. He looked pallid, white, as if he had been dusted with flour. He did not, in short, look like himself; he did not look alive. And Malcolm wished that he did not look so pale, wished, in other words, that he were not dead.[23] Perhaps he wondered if this whitened, powerless figure was really his father, wondered if his father was really dead.[24]

One further point may be made about the funeral. It was not Malcolm but Wilfred, his mother's favorite and one of the darkest skinned, who broke through the immobility of death to honor and protect his father, to keep the fly away from his defenseless face. Malcolm's feeling of guilt for not loving his mother and father sufficiently, as well as his sense of inadequacy when compared to his siblings, is captured in the passive role he thus assigns himself.

Before turning to the years between the death of Malcolm's father

[22] *Ibid.*

[23] It might be noted that comments on, and reactions to, skin color serve, throughout Malcolm's autobiography, as a language of emotion, a way of communicating what Malcolm and others are feeling.

[24] On warding off the consciousness of the death of a parent, see Martha Wolfenstein, "How Is Mourning Possible?" in *The Psychoanalytic Study of the Child,* Volume XXI, 1966.

and the time Malcolm left Michigan, a comparison with Churchill's reaction to his father's death is appropriate. Churchill, who at twenty was old enough to understand death, if not perhaps to accept it fully, knew his father was dying some months before his actual demise. While he, like Malcolm, had feelings of guilt in connection with the death, he also was able to manage those feelings by both manifestly and latently identifying with Lord Randolph. Malcolm's father, by contrast, died when Malcolm was much more exposed to feelings of guilt and inadequacy, when it was not yet possible for him both to identify with his father and to preserve his personal autonomy. As we shall see, he chose the path of rebellion: the "criminality" present in Churchill's school experiences was radically accentuated in Malcolm's youth and adolescence. It was a criminality that eventually called for redemption and martyrdom.

School Days

Malcolm, as was mentioned above, was always his mother's most troublesome child, at least as he remembers it. He was constantly fighting with his brothers, making a fuss until his mother gave him what he wanted, or yelling loudly if his mother threatened to hit him. Because his mother did not want other people to think she was abusing her child, this last tactic served to protect him when anyone outside the family was around.

Malcolm's behavior did not improve after his father's death. He reports that Wilfred quit school and got a job, and that an older sister started to do much more work around the house; but he goes on to say:

Philbert and I didn't contribute anything. We just fought all the time—each other at home, and then at school we would team up and fight white kids. Sometimes the fights would be racial in nature, but they might be about anything.[25]

Malcolm, at least retrospectively, blamed himself for not contributing to the family's welfare. Actually, he did use up some of his great energy catching frogs and shooting rabbits, both of which could be sold to provide a small supplement to the family's increasingly meager income. But, with the Depression tightening its grip on the country at large and poverty descending ever more rapidly on the Littles, Malcolm spent less time helping the family and doing his school work. As he put it: "The more I began to stay away from home and visit peo-

---

[25] Malcolm X, *The Autobiography* ..., p. 11.

ple and steal from stores, the more aggressive I became in my inclinations. I never wanted to wait for anything." [26]

Malcolm, in other words, was becoming more rebellious, more re-
sponsive to his aggressive impulses, and less receptive to constraint
and control. In this behavior he resembles Churchill, who also was
hard to manage and prone to disobey rules at this age. Both boys, we
might surmise, were misbehaving partly out of a sense of guilt and
partly out of hostility for the paternal figures who had, in one way or
another, deserted them.

The consequences of their misdemeanors were, however, quite different. Churchill, with his school authorities to restrain him and Mrs.
Everest's love to fall back upon, learned to direct his aggression into
socially accepted channels. Malcolm, lacking a substitute for his father
and having a mother who was collapsing mentally under the strain of
trying to maintain her large family, became sufficiently delinquent, by
the time he was thirteen, to be expelled from school and sent to a
detention home.

Malcolm's expulsion from school was only one more sign of his
family's progressive decay. Originally proud of their independence
and economic well-being, by 1934 the Littles were accepting welfare
payments and food supplements. Louise Little hated the state welfare people, who were white and who, according to Malcolm, were trying to break up the family:

[The welfare people] were as vicious as vultures. They had no feelings,
understanding, compassion or respect for my mother. They told us, "She's
crazy for refusing food." [She would not accept pork because of her dietary beliefs.] Right then was when our home, our unity, began to dis-
integrate. We were having a hard time, and I wasn't helping. But we could
have made it, we could have stayed together. As bad as I was, as much
trouble and worry as I caused my mother, I loved her.[27]

Whatever sins the welfare people may have been guilty of, it is himself that Malcolm is attacking under their name. He is accusing himself of being a vulture, of giving his mother so much trouble that
family unity was destroyed and she broke down under the pressure.

The unity of the family was destroyed not only emotionally but also
physically by the tribulations of poverty and the lack of a man in the
house. For a brief while, in 1935, things went well: "It was about this
time that the large, dark man from Lansing began visiting." [28] After

[26] *Ibid.,* p. 15.
[27] *Ibid.,* p. 18.
[28] *Ibid.*

about a year, he stopped coming by. Evidently he recoiled from the responsibility of managing the large and unruly Little brood. Now Malcolm's mother "began to sit around and walk around talking to herself—almost as though she was unaware that [the children] were there—it became increasingly terrifying." [29] What little love Malcolm was still receiving from his mother was thus rapidly being withdrawn.

Malcolm's ties to his mother were cut still further when he was sent to live with a more prosperous Negro family:

> When finally I was sent to the Gohannas' home, at least in a surface way I was glad. I remember that when I left home with the state man, my mother said one thing: "Don't let them feed him any pig." [30]

Eventually Malcolm was to honor his mother's command. For the moment he was glad to be where there was more food and a stable emotional environment. Yet, as he himself intimates, his sense of relief was superficial. His delinquent behavior continued, a good sign that he was still intent on calling attention to himself and punishing *both* parents for their neglect. In emulation of his older brother Philbert (and of Joe Louis), he tried to gain respect and love by becoming a boxer; but he lost his first two bouts to a white boy, which was a disgrace in itself and closed off this outlet for the release of aggression. Consequently, his "criminality" continued until the local authorities had him sent to a detention home.

It was largely as a result of the intervention of Mrs. Swerlin, the woman who ran the detention home, that Malcolm was not sent to a reform school. "Mrs. Swerlin was bigger than her husband . . . a big, buxom, robust, laughing woman"; in complete possession of her faculties and married to a man who was "quiet and polite," she was a striking contrast to Malcolm's mother. Malcolm, like the other boys, had his own room and ate with the Swerlins. He was impressed by the authority and fairness of this white woman, came to like her, and was liked in turn. The result was a temporary lessening of Malcolm's rebelliousness. Under Mrs. Swerlin's rather paternal guidance, he worked dutifully at a part-time job, was enrolled in the local junior high school, earned high grades, and was even elected class president.

The respite was, however, brief. Two experiences, coupled with the restlessness natural to adolescence, drew Malcolm away from rural Michigan and into the fast city life of Boston and New York.

In the spring of 1939, Malcolm's half-sister Ella came to visit. Ella,

[29] *Ibid.*
[30] *Ibid.*, p. 19.

one of Earl Little's children from his first marriage, was "a commanding woman, maybe even bigger than Mrs. Swerlin. . . ." She "wasn't just black, but, like our father, she was jet black." [31] And, Malcolm reports, "she was the first really proud black woman I had ever seen in my life. She was plainly proud of her very dark skin." [32] Ella, it is clear, evoked memories of her, and Malcolm's, father. In her Malcolm saw the same size, strength, and blackness that he had respected, and ambivalently loved, in his father. Ella was even able to make Malcolm's mother, who by this time was institutionalized in a mental hospital, momentarily calm and happy. In short, she possessed all the strong, loving qualities that Mrs. Swerlin did, and pride in her name and color in addition. When she offered Malcolm the opportunity to visit her in Boston that summer, it was not just the prospect of the big city that attracted him.

Malcolm was overwhelmed by Boston: "I couldn't have feigned indifference if I tried to. . . . I didn't know the world contained as many Negroes as I saw thronging downtown Roxbury at night. . . ." [33] Just as Ella had dwarfed Mrs. Swerlin, so Boston made Malcolm's hometown seem insignificant and dull. And perhaps Boston, with its multitude of Negroes—and Negroes who appeared to be at no man's beck and call—promised him an escape from the past and present, promised him a new identity and his father's power.

Malcolm was bored and restless when he returned to Mrs. Swerlin's home, but he continued to do well in school and stayed out of trouble. One day his English teacher, who prided himself on the advice he gave his students, asked Malcolm what kind of career he was planning. Malcolm, although he had not given the matter much thought, replied that he wanted to be a lawyer. His teacher was surprised, and told him to be realistic: "A lawyer," [he said], "that's no realistic goal for a nigger. . . . You're good with your hands—making things. . . . Why don't you plan on carpentry?" [34] In other words, Malcolm was told to remain a boy, to accept a lower status for himself than would white boys with comparable ability. He was being told, like Churchill, that he could not be a lawyer. But Churchill was given the alternative of a military career, a career that would utilize at least some of his talents and impulses. Malcolm's compliance with the rules of white society, by contrast, brought him only the prospect of occupational castration. When the school year ended,

[31] *Ibid.*, p. 33.
[32] *Ibid.*, p. 32.
[33] *Ibid.*, p. 34.
[34] *Ibid.*, p. 36.

therefore, Malcolm left Lansing and Mrs. Swerlin for Boston and
Ella's home in Roxbury.

Adolescence

Ostensibly Malcolm was going to Boston to live with Ella and accept her guidance; but the internal conflicts that made life with the
Swerlins intolerable similarly served to drive Malcolm away from the
loving, but domineering, Ella and the middle-class "Hill" section of
Roxbury and into the Boston ghetto, the "town." There he quickly
established a friendship with a young man he calls Shorty, who was
also from Lansing and decided to take Malcolm under his more
experienced wing. It was Shorty who got Malcolm his first job (as a
shoeshine boy at the Roseland Ballroom), told him where to get his
first "zoot suit," and gave him his first taste of heavy drinking and
marijuana. He also administered to Malcolm the most fundamental
rite de passage of "hip" manhood—he gave Malcolm his first "conk,"
or hair-straightening:

The congolene just felt warm when Shorty started coming it in. But
then my head caught on fire.
I gritted my teeth and tried to pull the sides of the kitchen table together. The comb felt as if it was raking my skin off.
My eyes watered, my nose was running. I couldn't stand it any longer;
I bolted to the washbasin. I was cursing Shorty with every name I could
think of when he got the spray going and started soap-lathering my head.[35]

Malcolm thus underwent a puberty rite not unlike the circumcision
rituals of many peoples and religions. He suffered the pain of a symbolic castration so that the adult members of the tribe, of the Negro
community in the "town," would recognize him as a peer. Later,
Malcolm was to reject this symbol of manhood and the style of life
it connoted. As he put it:

This was my first really big step toward self-degradation: when I en-
dured all of that pain, literally burning my flesh to have it look like a
white man's hair. I had joined the multitude of Negro men and women
in America who are brain-washed into believing that the black people
are "inferior"—and white people "superior"—that they will even violate
and mutilate their God-created bodies to try to look "pretty" by white
standards.[36]

[35] *Ibid.*, p. 53.
[36] *Ibid.*, p. 55.

For the moment, however, his "smooth sheen of shining red hair" and his flashy clothes had the desired effect. Once he learned to dance, to lindy-hop, he was one of the "coolest cats" around Roxbury. No one suspected that he was only fifteen, least of all the attractive white woman named Sophia who picked him up at a Roseland dance.

Sophia was to play an important part in Malcolm's life until he was sent to prison in 1946. Initially, she gave Malcolm "real status" around Roxbury:

With the best-looking white woman who ever walked in those bars and clubs, and with her giving me the money I spent, too, even the big, important black hustlers and "smart boys" ... were clapping me on the back ... and calling me "Red." Of course I knew their reason like I knew my own name: they wanted to steal my fine white woman away from me.[37]

While Malcolm was undoubtedly correct in thinking that his friends and acquaintances wanted his woman, he had other reasons for questioning their intentions, for the woman whom he had chosen, or rather who had chosen him, was taboo in more ways than one. From the viewpoint of the authorities of white society, the relationship was illicit because Malcolm was black. Malcolm might well anticipate that, if white men knew about it, they might try to end the liaison—or Malcolm's life. But Sophia must also have, at least unconsciously, reminded Malcolm of his mother. Light-skinned, attractive, and older than he was, she was also helping to support him. She was consequently forbidden by the laws of incest: his relationship with her carried with it the danger of castration, the son's punishment for succeeding too well in the oedipal rivalry with his father.

In 1941, Malcolm took a job selling sandwiches on trains running from Boston to other East Coast cities. Between trips he continued to see Sophia, but increasingly his life came to center around New York and the fast life in Harlem. From his first glimpse of New York he was "mesmerized" by the city: it "narcotized" him.[38] New York was "heaven" to him, and the center of heaven was Small's Paradise, one of the most popular night spots for the big-time hustlers, numbers operators, and other Harlem notables. In 1942, Malcolm got a job waiting tables in Small's.

For almost a year Malcolm worked in Small's by day and tasted the delights of Harlem by night. Here in "paradise" it seemed that

[37] *Ibid.*, p. 68.
[38] *Ibid.*, p. 75.

the doubts and fears that haunted him could be put to rest. He was no longer even Malcolm Little; instead, he was called Detroit Red, to differentiate him from two other red-haired Negroes who moved in the same circles. When he was working at Small's, there was a strict set of rules to keep his impulses in check and relieve him of the responsibility for making decisions: "No lateness, no laziness, no stealing, no kind of hustling off any customers, especially men in uniform." [39] And in the evenings he could quiet his conscience with good scotch whiskey and marijuana cigarettes.

In 1943, however, Malcolm managed to get expelled from paradise, just has he had severed, one way or another, his ties with his family, Mrs. Swerlin, Ella, and his friends, including Sophia, in Boston. The occasion was a spontaneous act of kindness which was also a violation of the rules: seeing a dejected looking soldier drinking in Small's, he asked him if he wanted a woman (many of the women who lived in Malcolm's apartment building were prostitutes). The soldier was a police spy, and Malcolm was repaid for his kindness by a warning from the police and the loss of his job at Small's.

Manifestly, it would appear that Malcolm was simply the victim of his own generous impulse. Yet he notes himself, that, as soon as he gave the prostitute's telephone number to the man, he knew something was wrong. Even before the police came to question him, he told one of the owners what he had done, suspecting that he had fallen into a trap. We might hypothesize, in other words, that Malcolm's feelings of guilt would not permit him to enjoy the relatively secure "family" life of Small's Paradise. He thus took the occasion of seeing the dejected soldier to break the rules and ensure his exile.[40]

Malcolm, at this point completely on his own, swung more decidedly than ever before away from compliance with the norms of white society and toward self-destruction. Just as when his father was killed he became increasingly unruly and hard to manage, so now he became genuinely criminal. He began by "hustling" marijuana; and, when the police started to close in on him, switched to working for Harlem racketeers running numbers and guiding white men to scenes of sexual perversion designed to appeal to them. He found it necessary to bury his anxieties and fears under heavy layers of drugs, including cocaine, and soon was staying "high"

---

[39] *Ibid.*, p. 80.

[40] To make the analogy fully explicit, it might be said that Adam, too, was ruined by success, that he was driven from his natal family, from the Garden of Eden, by the voice of his own conscience telling him he was a sinner.

throughout his waking hours. And he worked, then as later, an eighteen-hour day.

Gradually Malcolm started taking risks that were slightly too great and making mistakes in areas where one could not afford to make them. His increasing lack of control, in fact, so alarmed his friends that Shorty was called in to take him away from New York and out of circulation. Back in Boston, Malcolm rested only long enough to recover his physical and mental strength. In need of money, he formed a burglary ring consisting of Shorty, Sophia, another woman, and himself. At first successful and prudent, he soon grew careless. One day, while trying to have a stolen watch repaired, he was taken into custody, and, shortly thereafter, he was sent to prison. He was not quite twenty-one years old.

Malcolm's adolescence was thus very different from Churchill's. Churchill, living within the constraints of his family, Harrow, and Sandhurst, managed to keep his aggressive and self-destructive impulses within socially accepted bounds. Malcolm, without the support of his family or stabilizing social institutions, was not able to restrain either his impulses, or his feelings of guilt and self-condemnation in response to gratifying those impulses. Consequently his life oscillated between periods of self-control (and allowing himself to be controlled or guided by others) and times of wild emotional indulgence and self-destructive behavior. Yet, throughout these dangerous years, and despite the fact that he often carried a gun, Malcolm never killed another man. Churchill, as an officer in Her Majesty's Army, did.

Young Manhood

Malcolm entered Charlesworth State Prison in February, 1946. Deprived of both drugs and mobility for the first time in over five years, he was "physically miserable and as evil-tempered as a snake. . . ." [41] Malcolm had been running away from himself, from his sense of guilt or, to put it in religious terms, his feeling of sinfulness, since early adolescence. He had, with varying degrees of success, controlled his aggressive impulses by balancing self-destructive actions with achievement. Now he was without outlet for his hostile feelings, without an opportunity to keep moving, and without drugs. Hence he regressed to a posture of diffuse and childish rage, cursing everything and everyone that came close to him. Like a naughty child, he was uncooperative with his guards and spent much of his

[41] Malcolm X, *The Autobiography* . . . , p. 152.

first year in solitary confinement. His anger and hostility soon won him the nickname Satan.

Malcolm's rage during this year was, however, a sign not only of guilt and frustration but also of residual self-respect and unwillingness to accept his position. In this regard it is notable that one of Malcolm's techniques for defying his guards was to pretend to forget his number, his prison identity. In later years he was actually unable to recall (that is, he repressed) the number by which he was addressed every day that he was in prison. He was able to maintain, in other words, some sense of personal autonomy, even if it was the autonomy of Satan.

Yet he was very far from any kind of home, far from any feeling of being loved and sheltered. He was ripe for a doctrine that would promise him a return to paradise and a redemption from his sense of sin. If, however, he were to be able to escape the role of the devil, someone else would have to play it. If his hostility were not to be directed against himself, it would have to be directed toward someone else. His prison guards were natural objects of hatred, as they freely walked past his cell and ordered him around; but they were also representatives of the legal order against which Malcolm had sinned. It is thus not surprising that Elijah Muhammad's message that the prison guards were devils—and that the authority they represented was the devil incarnate—came upon Malcolm "like a blinding light." [42]

Malcolm's first contact with the Messenger's doctrine was in a letter from his favorite brother, Reginald, which said: "Don't eat pork, and don't smoke any more cigarettes. I'll show you the way to get out of prison." [43] Malcolm's response was to think that Reginald "had come upon some way I could work a hype on the penal authorities." [44] Unconsciously perhaps he felt that by not eating pork, by following his mother's dietary rules, he could belatedly win forgiveness for his aggressive sins. He did not, of course, realize that Reginald was promising him escape from the prison of his own "whitened" mind.[45]

Early in 1949 Reginald came to visit Malcolm and explained to him the rudiments of the Black Muslim creed. He told him that God

[42] *Ibid.,* p. 164. The parallel to Saint Paul's revelation on the road to Damascus is modestly observed by Malcolm himself on the preceding page.

[43] *Ibid.,* p. 155.

[44] *Ibid.*

[45] Concise presentations of Elijah Muhammad's ideology can be found in Chapter 11 of Malcolm's autobiography and Chapter 4 of Lincoln's *The Black Muslims in America.*

was a man who knew everything and that white men, all white men, were devils. Malcolm was confused, confused by the message itself and the layer of mystery that Reginald wove around it. God had 360 degrees of knowledge, he was told, and even the Masons, the most powerful devils, only had 33 degrees. Clearly Allah, the black man's god, was more powerful than the white devil—as powerful, we might add, as Earl Little must have appeared to his young son.

Malcolm had little trouble convincing himself that Allah, a god even more powerful than his father's Christian god, one that might protect him and other black men as his father's god had not been able to do, existed. But Malcolm had white friends as well as black ones; he remembered Mrs. Swerlin and others who had been good to him at one time or another. His prison guards might be devils, but how about these seemingly kindhearted people? His doubts were soon buried under the pseudohistory and pseudorationality of "Yacub's History," the demonology of the Lost-Found Nation of Islam in the West; a constant barrage of letters from various members of his family; and, finally, a letter from Elijah Muhammad himself telling him that "the black prisoner . . . symbolized white society's crime of keeping black men oppressed and deprived and ignorant, and unable to get decent jobs, turning them into criminals." [46]

Elijah Muhammad thus lifted the burden of personal guilt off Malcolm's shoulders and placed it upon those of white authority. He did this by permitting Malcolm to split the feelings of ambivalence toward his parents which had been plaguing him since early childhood. Instead of having mixed feelings for a father who was powerful, loving, and dangerous and a mother who was beloved and punitive, Malcolm could hate the white man with a clear conscience and love Elijah Muhammad (the "little, gentle, sweet man" who is also "the most powerful black man in America" [47]) fully and devotedly. He could be, at one and the same time, a scourge to his enemies and the Prophet's "slave . . . servant . . . [and] son." [48] For such a reward it would not be difficult to ignore those white men who did not appear to be properly devilish.

Viewed another way, his belief in Elijah Muhammad permitted Malcolm to begin life over again from age six. The Messenger could be felt to be a combined mother and father of the Black Muslim family; and Malcolm, instead of being an aggressive and rebellious

[46] Malcolm X, *The Autobiography* . . . , p. 100.

[47] *Ibid.*, p. 210.

[48] From an interview with Louis E. Lomax in Lomax, *When the Word Is Given* (New York: Signet Books, 1963), p. 179.

son who contributed to the disintegration of the family, could this time be loyal and obedient, this time would "bend [his] knees, admitting [his] guilt, to implore the forgiveness of God." [49] Thus Malcolm describes his "submission" to Allah while still in prison, his acceptance of his father's and mother's power and authority.

Once Malcolm accepted Elijah Muhammad as his guide, he wasted no time in trying to convince others to do the same. He wrote to almost everyone he knew in Harlem and Roxbury, trying to communicate to them the redemptive power of his newfound faith. Although he had no success while still in prison, he continued this "fishing" for converts after he was released. By so doing he proved his loyalty to the Prophet, gained a sense of the rectitude of his own beliefs by getting others to share them, and turned his passive acceptance of the faith into an active vocation. He discovered while still in prison, however, that his educational background was insufficient to permit him to communicate effectively to others in writing, and that even his speaking was limited to the vocabulary of the hustler's world. He therefore sent himself to school. He copied a dictionary page by page to improve his vocabulary and started to read omnivorously. Soon he found that he was able to win debates even against educated white men, and he resolved that his mission in life would be to tell "the white man about himself—or die." [50]

Malcolm, in other words, chose for himself the role of defender of the faith, the role in which his aggressive impulses could be gratified most fully. It is no wonder that, in introducing Elijah Muhammad to Muslim audiences, he would typically say:

I'm not going to take all day telling you some of the greatnesses of The Honorable Elijah Muhammad. I'm just going to tell you now his *greatest* greatness! He is the *first,* the *only* black leader to identify, to you and me, *who* is our enemy! [51]

When Malcolm was released from prison in 1952, he went to live with his brother Wilfred in Detroit. The "warmth" of Muslim family life had a "healing" effect on him; [52] his surmise while still in prison that within the Nation he would find a home was thus confirmed. Soon his devotion to the Nation attracted the attention of Elijah Muhammad; and Malcolm X, now a Muslim and no longer Malcolm

[49] Malcolm X, *The Autobiography* ..., p. 170.
[50] *Ibid.,* p. 185.
[51] *Ibid.,* p. 251.
[52] *Ibid.,* p. 193.

Little or Detroit Red, became a minister. As mentioned in the first part of this chapter, Malcolm used that ministry to transform the Muslims and himself from marginal members of black urban life to one of the most respected and feared forces in American society. The Nation thus provided Malcolm with a family he could love; a home that would shelter him; the impetus for self-education and the textbooks out of which he learned; a vocation to which his energy, rhetorical skills, and aggressive impulses could be legitimately applied; and a God, a Prophet, a father whom he could loyally serve. The Muslims provided, in other words, a reconstituted world which replaced the damaged and intolerable one of Malcolm's youth and adolescence.

By 1962, however, there were signs of corruption even in this paradise. First, Malcolm learned what others had long known, that his Prophet, the embodiment of black strength and morality, had been having sexual relations with his secretaries, two of whom ultimately brought him to court on paternity charges. In the past, Malcolm had "refused to accept anything so grotesque as adultery mentioned in the same breath with Mr. Muhammad's name." [53] Eventually, however, the evidence became overwhelming, and Malcolm was tormented: he, who had been the smartest "hustler" in Harlem, had been duped—by the man who had "virtually raised [him] from the dead." [54] Then Malcolm learned that Elijah Muhammad had often told his secretaries that, while Malcolm was the best minister he had ever had, he was also "dangerous" and would turn against the Prophet some day. Malcolm was deeply hurt and, as he reports it, "I felt almost out of my mind." [55]

Malcolm had accepted Elijah Muhammad with a truly filial love; he had trusted him as one ideally trusts one's father; and it was the Prophet who had given him, if not life itself, at least rebirth, a new name, and something approaching psychic harmory. Now it appeared that the man whose love was his ultimate reward preferred sexual indulgence to the pure relationship of father and son. Malcolm writes of his reactions when he learned that Elijah Muhammad not only did not love him, but desired him dead:

I was in a state of emotional shock. I was like someone who for twelve years had had an inseparable, beautiful marriage—and then suddenly one morning at breakfast the marriage partner had thrust across the table some divorce papers.

[53] *Ibid.,* p. 295.
[54] *Ibid.,* p. 296.
[55] *Ibid.,* p. 297.

I felt as though something in *nature* had failed, like the sun, or the stars. . . .[56]

Malcolm's description of his feelings makes it clear that he was emotionally wedded to Elijah Muhammad, that he loved him as one loves father, mother, and wife.

Just as shattering as Elijah Muhammad's hostility was the Prophet's suspicion that Malcolm would someday betray him. Malcolm, whose unconscious guilt had driven him to criminality in the past and who was in fact beginning to find Elijah Muhammad's rules restrictive (in particular, Malcolm craved more active political involvement, enlarged opportunities for combat, than the Prophet would permit), could not easily reject this accusation, at least not unconsciously. It is the return of his sense of sinfulness, of his feelings of guilt, to which we may attribute his inner turmoil at this time. In his words: "My head felt like it was bleeding inside. I felt like my brain was damaged." [57] For his sins against the father he was being punished with Earl Little's death agony.

By early 1964 the break between Malcolm and Elijah Muhammad was complete. In a sense, Malcolm in his late thirties was emerging from a delayed and prolonged latency and adolescence. He was thus in much the same emotional position as was Churchill after the death of Lord Randolph. And both men responded to their separations from paternal authority by intensified identification. Churchill, as we have seen, eagerly read his father's speeches and sought to absorb his political style; Malcolm, through his pilgrimage to Mecca, tried to establish for himself Elijah Muhammad's relationship to the father in heaven. And through his creation of the Organization of Afro-American Unity, he tried to duplicate the Prophet's—and his father's—relationship to men who would follow and believe in him.

As Churchill's leap from the bridge shows, however, adolescence is a dangerous, guilt-ridden, and self-destructive time. Malcolm, whose conscience plagued him far more than did Churchill's, was not able to defend himself adequately against his own aggressive impulses. He knew that there were men trying to kill him every time he appeared in public. Yet he refused to take even the most rudimentary protective measures against the former father and brothers who were stalking him. Rather in death he would prove his ultimate devotion to his father and to the family he now sought to serve, the family of man:

[56] *Ibid.,* p. 304.
[57] *Ibid.,* p. 303.

I'm glad to be free of [the Black Muslims]. It's a time for martyrs now. And if I'm to be one, it will be for the cause of brotherhood. That's the only thing that can save this country. I've learned it the hard way—but I've learned it. . . .[58]

The Personality of the Adherent

Leaders and Followers

Adherents of a cause such as Malcolm X are political men no less than leaders such as Winston Churchill. We are therefore not surprised that Harold Lasswell's formulation, that political men displace private motives onto public objects and rationalize them in terms of the public interest, applies equally well to both. For both men, moreover, the underlying motive that predisposed them to political participation was the need to manage their ambivalent feelings toward their fathers in particular and their families in general. Churchill accomplished this task by identifying with Lord Randolph in the latter's role as political leader. Malcolm, by contrast, selected the role of loyal son to a powerful political and religious father.

More specifically, Malcolm tried to minimize his internal conflicts by living in a sharply bifurcated world. His love for his father was displaced onto Elijah Muhammad; his hatred of Earl Little, onto the white devil. This splitting of ambivalence was justified and made plausible by the Prophet's message, which presumed to give a divine and rational explanation of all human history, past, present, and future. In so doing it defined not only Malcolm's relationship to his father, but also provided him with beloved and loving Muslim brothers and sisters to replace the family of his childhood, and with enemies toward whom he could direct his hostile feelings.

Thus both Churchill and Malcolm X used the public world as an arena for the gratification of their emotional needs. Both, in addition, developed skills appropriate to that sphere. Malcolm, from early adolescence on, practiced the art of selling, of "hustling." At first a hustler of shoeshines at Roseland, he was eventually to sell, to preach, redemption to his fellow black men and a message of guilt and shame to white men. Churchill developed military skills, as well as the oratorical talents appropriate to the House of Commons.

Yet Malcolm, unlike Churchill, allowed another man to dictate to him what he should believe, what he should say, and how he should act. This, of course, is the essence of adherency, of followership. By briefly retracing in theoretical terms the path that led him to this

[58] *Ibid.,* p. 429.

position, we shall gain some understanding of the personality of the adherent, the true believer.

Escape from Freedom [59]

For the follower, the sense of guilt that accompanies aggressive thoughts and actions is so great that restraint and direction, emotional control, is sought outside the individual's own personality. A leader is desired who will lift the burden of free choice, which is also the possibility of sinning, from his shoulders. Without this escape from responsibility for his actions, the potential follower feels, at least unconsciously, that even his everyday accomplishments are aggressive, blameworthy, or worthless. This feeling leads him to destroy or devalue what he achieves for himself, and often inclines him to seek punishment in genuine criminality.

In Malcolm's case, the original "accomplishment" that tainted his subsequent actions was the death of his father. Unconsciously, we have surmised, Malcolm hated the father he also loved; and this hostility resulted in feelings of guilt when his father was killed. By his increasing delinquency after his father's death, he was both admitting his guilt and attempting to direct his hostility away from himself. The disintegration of his family and his sentencing to reform school were the punishments he thereby earned. At this point, having gained the aggressive release and punishment he craved, Malcolm was again ready to be a loyal son. Mrs. Swerlin and then Ella were both powerful and loving enough to win his temporary respect and submission. But submitting to their direction also meant that Malcolm had to accept a passive role analogous to the one he had with his father. Hence rejection of these reconstituted families became necessary, for being a good boy, a dutiful family member, carried with it the threat of emasculation.

As we have seen, Malcolm repeated this pattern in first obeying and then violating the rules of Small's Paradise. He was caught in an increasingly self-destructive oscillation between compliance and criminality. Underlying this cycle was his ambivalence toward his father: both rebellion against and submission to authority brought feelings of guilt and the fear of castration, feelings he tried to drown in restless mobility and drugs. Eventually his criminality resulted in

[59] This phrase is taken from Erich Fromm's *Escape from Freedom* (New York: Holt, Rinehart and Winston, 1941). Further development of the themes Fromm introduced in that work, themes that underlie much of this chapter, can be found in T. W. Adorno *et al., The Authoritarian Personality* (New York: Harper & Bros., 1950).

symbolic castration, for his imprisonment deprived him of his drugs, his mobility, and his name.

Thus Malcolm's attempt to win manhood for himself, to channel his energies in productive ways, ended in failure. He was not able, as was Churchill, to work out for himself an adaptative public identity, to displace his motives from his family to the political world. It took the intervention of a substitute father, Elijah Muhammad, to make this possible. Only by submitting to the Prophet, by yielding to him the prerogative for all judgments and decisions, was Malcolm able to escape his feelings of guilt. Only by accepting the role of Elijah Muhammad's son and allowing himself to be absorbed into the family of Islam was he able to cast off his sense of impotence, of powerlessness. And only by fighting the Prophet's battles and doing his work was he able to direct his aggressive impulses away from himself and link them to militant political tasks. Elijah Muhammad gave him, in short, the gift of belief, of a holy cause to serve.

Political leaders, it is true, are often the servants of a cause. Churchill was as devoted to England as Malcolm was to the Nation of Islam, but Churchill was able to serve his country as a father serves his children. His identification with Lord Randolph and his relatively manageable feelings of guilt allowed him to accept responsibility and freedom in a way Malcolm could not. He did not need therefore what the adherent needs, the emotional support of a substitute father and a closely knit band of brothers.

Devout adherency has its social, as well as its psychological, aspects. Malcolm's need for Elijah Muhammad's guidance was as much a product of racial injustice as it was of the particular circumstances of his family experience. Churchill's birthright was an aristocratic name and a well-structured social environment. Malcolm had to deal with the facelessness of black men in a white society and the chaos of a childhood disrupted by violence, death, and family disintegration. Viewed against this background, it is not surprising that Elijah Muhammad's message was appealing to Malcolm. Rather it is Malcolm's self-overcoming, his determined struggle for an independent manhood, that is both surprising and worthy of admiration.

The Political Group [60]

In discussing leaders we noted that one of their distinguishing characteristics is the lack of deep emotional ties to other human

---

[60] This section is based on Freud's *Group Psychology and the Analysis of the Ego* (*Standard Ed.*, 18). The generalizations it contains, like those in Freud's analysis, are meant to apply only to groups that demand a total commitment from their adherents.

beings. The adherent, by contrast, is very much the member of a group. He is emotionally bound to both his leader and his fellow adherents. According to Freud's original formulation of the point, "A primary group of this kind is a number of individuals who have put one and the same object in the place of their ego ideal and have consequently identified themselves with one another in their ego." [61] In other words, the member of a group substitutes the moral imperatives of a leader for the dictates of his own conscience. He places himself in the position of a son with respect to a powerful father. At the same time he gains a sense of similarity, of having an important part of the self in common, with the other members. They, too, are the father's sons.

Several important consequences follow from this double identificatory bond. First, as we have already seen in Malcolm's case, giving moral responsibility to a leader frees an adherent from his sense of guilt. He shifts onto the leader's shoulders not only the burden of current ethical choice, but also the consequences of past sins as well. Looked at another way, leaders of groups like the Nation of Islam, or, say, the Bolsheviks, are redeemers. They all perform the fundamental religious function of relieving their followers of their unconscious feelings of guilt.

Aside from shouldering the load of moral judgment, leaders help to reduce their adherents' sense of guilt by making possible the legitimated expression of aggressive impulses. Men like Malcolm are plagued by their own hostilities. They need an enemy, someone toward whom they can direct the hostility they feel for paternal authority and for themselves. They need an escape from ambivalence, a clear division of the world into friend and foe. This, too, their leaders provide. Elijah Muhammad's "greatest greatness," as Malcolm put it, was to tell the black man who his enemy was. He gave Malcolm someone he could feel justified in fighting.

Adherents gain from their leaders and their fellows not only a definition of the enemy, but also an outlet for their feelings of affection and love. They have the privilege and obligation of loving their leader as one does a father and loving their comrades as one would want to be loved by them. This object relationship complements and reinforces the identification with the leader and with fellow adherents that, as Freud inferred, also exists. By identification the leader has become a part of the follower's personality, a part that draws the respect that would otherwise be given to his conscience. Similarly the member feels that he is alive as long as his brothers live, and that they are alive in him.

[61] *Ibid.*, p. 116.

It is thus clear that true believers, adherents of groups like the Muslims, negate their individual identities in favor of a more powerful collective one. In so doing, however, they also surrender the right and the ability to apply the powers of reason or criticism to any basic aspect of the collectivity. In order to preserve the reconstituted family of the political group, the emotional outlets and support that give them their feelings of self-worth, rectitude, and importance, they must accept without question the decisions of the leader and the consensus of the group as a whole. It might here be mentioned that nations in time of war tend to resemble political groups like the Muslims in this respect, as well as in their proclivity for seeing everything in kill-or-be-killed terms.

While the filial position of an adherent severely hampers his ability to apply his critical faculties, it does not eliminate the thinking process altogether. In response to the need of followers to have a structure of words to justify and explain the group's actions, or in response to their own needs for explanation and justification, leaders develop or adopt at least a crude ideology. Such ideologies may be more or less realistic, more or less useful for making behavioral predictions or dealing successfully with other people. For most adherents, however, they need only appear to be rational, they need only appear to be scientific or empirically accurate; for, given the emotional needs of the adherent, a web of rationalizations which describes the world as the individual wishes to see it, which tells him that he is good and his enemies, evil, is almost certain to be more convincing than a carefully worked out empirical theory that does not provide a satisfactory outlet for his feelings.

Another aspect of ideologies such as the one developed by Elijah Muhammad is that their fixity is more important than their scientific utility. Because the political group provides its members with psychic peace only by distorting and restructuring the natural ambivalence of the personality, unambiguous and rigid formulas are needed to keep mixed feelings and guilt from recurring. Hence all such movements develop their codes of conduct and canonical books.

These ideologies, it might be mentioned, are not identical with fully developed political philosophies. In fact, they are typically vulgarizations of more sophisticated intellectual productions. Nonetheless it should be stressed that both highly articulated philosophies and crudely elaborated ideologies serve the unconscious needs of their originators and adherents. Both, moreover, contain rationalizations as well as reason. They differ from each other not in kind but in degree.

4

Political Philosophers

In one of the most famous passages in *Thus Spoke Zarathustra*, Nietzsche evokes the mental state of a man obsessed by guilt, of a "pale criminal":

An image made this pale man pale. He was equal to his deed when he did it; but he could not bear its image after it was done. Now he always saw himself as the doer of one deed. Madness I call this ... madness *after* the deed I call this.[1]

In this chapter it will be argued that the pale criminal was Nietzsche himself; that his analysis of Christian morality was, in part, an attempt to eradicate his own unconscious sense of guilt, and to vindicate through repetition the aggressive "deeds" of his childhood; and that his linked conceptions of eternal recurrence, the will to power, and the overman (*übermensch*) were the guarantors of this effort.[2]

Nietzsche, we should note, is not usually considered to be a political philosopher. He did not participate in governmental activity, he seldom wrote directly about the state, and no ideology is immediately deducible from his views.[3] Consequently, if one defines

---

[1] Friedrich W. Nietzsche, *Thus Spoke Zarathustra*, Part 1, "On the Pale Criminal," in Walter Kaufmann, ed., *The Portable Nietzsche* (New York: The Viking Press, 1954), p. 150.

[2] See Walter Kaufmann's treatment of these concepts in his *Nietzsche: Philosopher, Psychologist, Antichrist* (New York: Meridian Books, 1956), Part III.

[3] The one effort to transform the will to power into power politics and Nietzsche's attack on all values into anti-Semitism—by the Nazis—was based upon gross distortions of Nietzsche's views.

politics by such criteria, Nietzsche would not be a political man. Our definition, by contrast, demands only that a political philosopher be primarily oriented to questions of power and authority. In these terms Nietzsche, who believed that even the creation of God's authority was a manifestation of the will to power, was decidedly political.[4] And we shall see that, as the notion of the pale criminal implies, Nietzsche's concern with power and authority derived from impulses similar to those that led Churchill and Malcolm X to enter public life.

There are, of course, important differences between Nietzsche and the other two men. Both his way of thinking and style of living were far removed from those of the activists. Because they were, because Nietzsche was archetypically a philosopher, an examination of some aspects of his life should help us to see clearly the differences between the thinker and the activist.

Friedrich Nietzsche as Political Philosopher: "God Is Dead" [5]

Let us discuss some of the salient features of political philosophies and then turn to a consideration of the lives of philosophers. For heuristic purposes, we may think of philosophies as having three general aspects. First, any philosophy has its fundamental, and ultimately metaphysical, assumptions. Second, derived from, or at least framed by, these assumptions will be a set of relatively concrete hypotheses about power and authority. Third, a particular style of thought, method and way of using language will link these assumptions and hypotheses into a more or less integrated theory.

In many ways, Nietzsche's style of thought was his most distinctive attribute. Although both early and late in his career he constructed straightforward syllogistic arguments, he was also a master of argument by aphorism, a lover of dithyrambic poetry, and a skilled poser of paradoxes. His first major works, *The Birth of Tragedy Out of the Spirit of Music* (1872) and the *Untimely Meditations* (1873–1876), were in fairly conventional essay form. The first part of *Human, All-Too-Human* (1878) began the transition to a more

---

[4] In fact, it is not too much to say that one of Nietzsche's contributions to contemporary political thought was to extend the domain of politics to its furthest limit, to the point where existence itself becomes politics.

[5] Nietzsche's most famous elaboration of this theme is in the parable of the madman in *The Gay Science*. See Kaufmann, *The Portable Nietzsche*, p. 95.

aphoristic, fragmentary, and, as Nietzsche put it, "experimental" style. Nietzsche had always been able to turn a striking phrase; now the phrases took on independent life:

THE LIMITS OF UPRIGHTNESS.—Even the most upright author lets fall a word too much when he wishes to round off a period.
THE BEST AUTHOR.—The best author will be he who is ashamed to become one.[6]

As these aphorisms show, Nietzsche was very sensitive to questions of style, including his own. He thought, moreover, that the age in which he lived lacked taste and power, that is produced fragments instead of completed works, pedestrian scholarship instead of intellectual adventure. (This observation has been repeated so many times since, especially in American academia, that it is no longer even untimely!)

Nietzsche's avowed purpose in turning to a fragmentary and aphoristic style was to confront and overcome his own philosophic "decadence."[7] What other men did from cowardice and a failure of will, he would do from boldness. Thus *Miscellaneous Maxims and Opinions* (1879) and *The Wanderer and His Shadow* (1880), which Nietzsche treated as sequels to *Human, All-Too-Human*, constitute a veritable explosion of planned disorder.[8]

Nietzsche's next two works, *The Dawn of Day* (1881) and *The Gay Science* (1882) developed further his experimental or decadent style. Nietzsche's tone became, however, increasingly rhapsodic, increasingly prophetic and exhortative. Then, between 1883 and 1885, *Thus Spoke Zarathustra* came into being. Zarathustra, or Zoroaster, was a Persian prophet who taught a dualistic religious creed. In Nietzsche's hands he becomes a wandering teacher of the coming of the *übermensch*. Accordingly Nietzsche was, at this time, frankly allegorical and poetic. What had been aphorisms and insights in his earlier works were transformed into visions and parables. Virtually all literary forms were here blended, very much in the manner of Richard Wagner's attempt to create a total art, a unified combination of music, drama, and setting. Indeed, Zarathustra is both a "dancer"

[6] Friedrich W. Nietzsche, *Human, All-Too-Human* (London: George Allen & Unwin Ltd., 1909), I, 180.

[7] See Kaufmann's discussion of this and related points in his *Nietzsche: Philosopher, Psychologist, Antichrist*, Chap. 2.

[8] Nietzsche, like Hamlet, warns his listeners that there is method in his madness: "AGAINST THE SHORT-SIGHTED.—Do you think it is piece-work because it is (and must be) offered you in pieces?" From *Miscellaneous Maxims and Opinions*, in *Human, All-Too-Human* (New York: The Macmillan Company, 1924), II, 69.

and the hero of a drama; correspondingly, Nietzsche's style became musical and heroic as never before.

Beyond Good and Evil (1886) and the other works of Nietzsche's final creative period are less rhapsodic than *Thus Spoke Zarathustra*, less aphoristic than the works preceding this great philosophical allegory and somewhat less continuous than his earliest essays; rather they constitute an attempted integration of Nietzsche's earlier stylistic experiments.[9] In his last works, however, his tendency to become bombastic and overly assertive, to sound strident instead of compelling, is more pronounced. Even Nietzsche's first works are often a little too loud, a little too emphatic; his last ones are markedly so.

We have already alluded to Nietzsche's penchant for contradiction and paradox. So striking, in fact, is this aspect of his work that Karl Jaspers has noted that all of Nietzsche's statements "seem to be annulled by other statements." [10] Nietzsche loved to contradict himself both in substance and in form, and challenged his readers to find the unity behind the contradiction. Thus, for example, the first part of *Zarathustra* is cast in biblical form. It begins with a hymn to the sun, and Zarathustra's first words to the world at large are an exhortation: "*I teach you the overman.* Man is something that shall be overcome. What have you done to overcome him?" [11] Yet, at the end of the first part, Zarathustra says to his disciples: "Go away from me and resist Zarathustra! And even better: be ashamed of him! Perhaps he deceived you." [12] In *Ecce Homo* (1888), his autobiographical description of "how one becomes what one is," [13] Nietzsche comments:

In every word [Zarathustra] contradicts, this most Yes-saying of all spirits; in him all opposites are blended into a new unity.... The psychological problem in the type of Zarathustra is how he that says No and *does* No to an unheard-of degree, to everything to which one has so far said Yes, can nevertheless be the opposite of a No-saying spirit.[14]

---

[9] In addition to *Ecce Homo* (discussed below) and two anti-Wagnerian polemics, Nietzsche wrote *Towards a Genealogy of Morals, Twilight of the Idols,* and *The Antichrist* before insanity overtook him in January, 1889. *The Will of Power* was put together from his notes after his death in 1900.

[10] Karl Jaspers, *Nietzsche* (Tucson: The University of Arizona Press, 1965), p. 10.

[11] Nietzsche, *Thus Spoke Zarathustra,* in Kaufmann, *The Portable Nietzsche,* p. 124.

[12] *Ibid.,* p. 190.

[13] Friedrich W. Nietzsche, *Ecce Homo,* in Walter Kaufmann, ed., *On the Genealogy of Morals and Ecce Homo* (New York: Vintage Books, 1967), p. 215.

[14] *Ibid.,* pp. 305–306.

Nietzsche himself intimates, in the first words of *Ecce Homo*, where the solution to the "psychological problem" of Zarathustra lies:

> The good fortune of my existence, its uniqueness perhaps, lies in its fatality: I am, to express it in the form of a riddle, already dead as my father, while as my mother I am still living and becoming old.[15]

Part of our task in this chapter is, therefore, to attempt to solve this riddle, to come to an understanding of the paradoxical style of Nietzsche's thought. In the process we will also consider the development of this style and Nietzsche's tendency to overstate his arguments.

Nietzsche's use of paradox and experimentation as his method of argument does not, of course, exist independently of his substantive concerns. His changes in style were designed to express most accurately changes and variations in his thoughts and moods:

> To communicate a state, an inward tension of pathos, by means of signs, including the tempo of these signs—that is the meaning of every style; and considering that the multiplicity of inward states is exceptionally large in my case, I have many stylistic possibilities. . . .[16]

Let us accordingly turn our attention to Nietzsche's development of his fundamental assumptions and some of the more concrete hypotheses of his philosophy. At the same time we may consider the changes in his life circumstances that accompanied his variation of philosophic style and content.

The Birth of Tragedy and the *Untimely Meditations* were written while Nietzsche was a professor of classical philology at the University of Basel, Switzerland. At this time he was a loyal adherent of Wagner's musical drama and Schopenhauer's philosophy of the will. Together these two visions sheltered him and gave him both guidance and fellowship. The guidance came from Wagner himself, with whom Nietzsche was intimate during those years; and the fellowship came from other young men who also deemed Wagner to be the Schopenhauerian word made flesh. In fact, Nietzsche in the 1870s was in a position of discipleship similar to that of Malcolm X during his Black Muslim phase. Wagner and the Wagnerians were

---

[15] *Ibid.*, p. 222.

[16] *Ibid.*, p. 265. Nietzsche goes on to argue that *"Good* is any style that really communicates an inward state. . . . Good style *in itself*—a pure folly, mere "idealism," on a level with the "beautiful in itself," the "good in itself," the "thing in itself."

virtually his only friends; articulate loyalty to the cause, his ultimate justification and reason for being.

The relatively orthodox, at least for Nietzsche, style of these essays thus reflects the young philosopher's devotion to an established (although not then popular) philosophic-aesthetic vision and the demands of his academic station. In content, too, they are the works of a disciple, a true believer, albeit an original one. Just as Malcolm X sought to extend and consolidate Elijah Muhammad's power, so Nietzsche worked for a Wagnerian hegemony in German intellectual life.

The Birth of Tragedy is both an exercise in Schopenhauerian aesthetics and a panegyric to Wagner. Nietzsche argues that Greek tragedy, and the way of life that sustained it, was grounded in a delicate union of Dionysiac (irrational, willful, emotional, and musical) and Apollonian (ideational, artistic, and dream-creating) forces:

Dionysos speaks the language of Apollo, but Apollo, finally, the language of Dionysos; thereby the highest goal of tragedy and of art in general is reached.[17]

These two forces interacting thus create a new form, a synthesis, that transcends each of them. Tragedy in turn, however, is destroyed—by Socratism. Socrates, the arch-sophist, is viewed as trying to subordinate instinct entirely to reason. The resulting overemphasis on intellect, in which "instinct is the critic, consciousness the creator," is a "monstrosity."[18] And this monstrosity has ruled and perverted western man down to the present day, when at long last Wagnerian opera portends a new tragic age. This age, Nietzsche hoped, would be a higher synthesis of the Apollonian and the Dionysiac, for which "the music-practicing Socrates might be a fitting symbol."[19]

In the *Untimely Meditations* Nietzsche continues in the role of disciple. The first two, *David Strauss, the Confessor and Writer* and *On the Use and Disadvantage of History for Life*, are attacks on the "Philistine" quality of contemporary German culture, a culture that did not yet honor Wagner or acknowledge the authority of Schopenhauer. The next two, *Schopenhauer as Educator* and *Richard Wagner*

---

[17] Friedrich W. Nietzsche, *The Birth of Tragedy,* in Francis Goffling, ed., *The Birth of Tragedy and The Genealogy of Morals* (Garden City, New York: Doubleday Anchor Books, 1956), p. 131.

[18] *Ibid.*, p. 84.

[19] *Ibid.*, p. 105.

at Bayreuth (the newly erected center for the performance of Wagnerian opera), propose that the former is essentially the ideal philosopher, and the latter, the ideal artist.

By this time, however, the period of Nietzsche's orthodoxy was
drawing to a close. Wagner was becoming a national hero in the late
1870s, accepting the worship of the Philistines Nietzsche despised;
Schopenhauer no longer seemed to possess all the answers; academic
life was becoming increasingly onorous; and Nietzsche's health, which
had always been delicate, had now become decidedly poor. In 1876,
Nietzsche fled from the scene of Wagner's triumph at Bayreuth and
took a leave of absence from his university position.

Between 1876 and 1883, Nietzsche moved restlessly from place
to place, from idea to idea, and from style to style. His peace of mind
diminished; his loneliness and ill-health almost overwhelmed him.
It was during this time that he did his experimental or decadent
writing. Just as he shifted location and medication to try to find
relief from the nausea, insomnia, and near-blindness that were his
almost constant companions, so he experimented feverishly with the
form and content of his writings. He was looking for a vision to replace the one he had lost, a new guarantor of his moral and artistic
existence. He wrote:

Doubt devours me. I have killed the Law, and now the Law haunts me as
a cadaver haunts a living person. If I am not more than the Law, then I
am among the damned souls the most damned.[20]

As this passage intimates, in his quest Nietzsche had turned his
attention increasingly toward questions of morality, specifically
Christian morality. His "campaign against morality," as he later
described it in *Ecce Homo*, began in *The Dawn* and was further developed in *The Gay Science*. In these works, Nietzsche treats Christianity as a latter-day analogue to Socratism, undermining Roman
nobility as Socratism had destroyed the tragic spirit.[21]

Now, however, Christianity was being undermined in turn; even
the "herd," the natural adherents of Christian morality, was becoming atheistic. Nietzsche, in the prophetic guise of "the madman,"
gives voice to the anguish of living in a Godless world:

[20] Quoted by Kurt F. Reinhardt in his introduction to Friedrich W. Nietzsche,
The Joyful Wisdom [or *The Gay Science*] (New York: Frederick Ungar Publishing Co., 1960), p. 5.

[21] See, for example, sections 55–96 of *The Dawn*. Or, as Nietzsche states his
views more concisely in section 98: "ALTERATIONS IN MORALS.—Morals are
constantly undergoing changes and transformations, occasioned by successful
crimes. . . ."

"Whither is God" he cried. "I shall tell you. *We have killed him*—you and I. . . . But how have we done this? How were we able to drink up the sea? . . . What did we do when we unchained this earth from its sun? Whither is it moving now? Away from all suns? Are we not plunging continually? . . . Is there any up or down left? . . . Has it not become colder? . . . Do we not hear anything yet of the noise of the gravediggers who are burying God? . . . God is dead. God remains dead. And we have killed him. How shall we, the murderers of all murderers, comfort ourselves? What was holiest and most powerful of all that the world has yet owned has bled to death under our knives . . . . What will wipe this blood off us? . . . Is not the greatness of this deed too great for us? Must not we ourselves become gods simply to seem worthy of it? . . .[22]

Nietzsche, by abandoning the worship of all established values, thus found himself in the same position as Malcolm X after his break with the Prophet. Malcolm's response to the dilemma of damaged faith was to appeal to Allah; Nietzsche's was to create a new vision of the cosmos, a new God, and a new prophet for that God. Thus at the end of *The Gay Science*, in a section entitled "The Tragedy Begins," Zarathustra is born.

The key to Nietzsche's new faith was the idea of eternal recurrence, the first discovery or assumption that frames his mature thought. Just before the reference to Zarathustra in *The Gay Science* he wrote:

What if a demon crept after thee into thy loneliest loneliness some day or night, and said to thee: "This life, as thou livest it at present, and hast lived it, thou must live it once more, and also innumerable times. . . .[23]

How might one respond to this demon? With despair or with gaiety? The posing of this question, Nietzsche believed, constituted the breaking point, the "great noon," of human history; for he who answered it with gaiety, he who affirmed the value of life in the face of its eternal recurrence, would thereby also condemn and negate all previous values, especially all otherwordly values. Affirmation of life, affirmation of man and what man could become, would replace the worship of God or nihilistic despair. Here, then, was the basic presupposition of what Nietzsche was increasingly to term his "revaluation of all values."

The idea of eternal recurrence came to Nietzsche in August, 1881, during the first of the euphoric moods that recurred intermittently throughout the 1880s. The first part of *Zarathustra*, in which that

[22] In Kaufmann, *The Portable Nietzsche*, pp. 95–96.
[23] Nietzsche, *The Joyful Wisdom*, p. 270.

germ bore fruit, was not written until February, 1883. In *Ecce Homo* Nietzsche notes that it took "eighteen months for the pregnancy," and that Zarathustra was born "exactly in that sacred hour in which Richard Wagner died in Venice." [24] In the intervening months Nietzsche had a painful relationship with a young Russian woman, Lou Andreas-Salome. This young woman was fascinated by Nietzsche's ideas but was not attracted to him romantically. She therefore refused his shy proposal of marriage, and Nietzsche was more than ever condemned to living alone.

From this point forward, Nietzsche's life was one of almost unbroken solitude and substantial physical misery. During the euphoric moods mentioned above, he gave birth, between 1883 and 1888, to his greatest works, all of which are grounded in the affirmation of life through eternal recurrence, the assumption of a universal will to power, and the prophecy of the *übermensch.*

The will to power is to eternal recurrence as essence is to existence. It is the underlying dynamus of all action, the animating force of both individual and cultural life. "Life as such is will to power," Nietzsche says in *Beyond Good and Evil;* and in *Zarathustra* he proclaims:

A tablet of good hangs over every people. Behold, it is the tablet of their overcomings; behold, it is the voice of their will to power.[25]

Later in the book he goes on to say:

Where I found the living, there I found will to power; and even in the will of those who serve I found the will to be master. . . .

And life itself confided this secret to me: "Behold," it said, "I am *that which must always overcome itself.* . . .

Verily, I say unto you: good and evil that are not transitory, do not exist. Driven on by themselves, they must overcome themselves again and again. . . .

And whoever must be a creator in good and evil, he must be an annihilator and break values. . . .[26]

The will to power of any organism is thus the drive of that organism to transform itself into something higher, something beyond what it already is. All that was and is, is preparation for what will be. Man

[24] Nietzsche, *Ecce Homo,* in Kaufmann, ed., *On the Genealogy of Morals and Ecce Homo,* p. 295. He goes on to remark: "This figure of exactly eighteen months might suggest, at least to Buddhists, that I am really a female elephant."

[25] "On the Thousand and One Goals," in Kaufmann, ed., *The Portable Nietzsche,* p. 170.

[26] "On Self-Overcoming," *Ibid.,* pp. 226–228.

himself is accordingly a preparation for, a bridge to, the beyond man, the higher man, ultimately the *übermensch*. And Zarathustra, who is preparing the way for the *übermensch*, must, therefore, be an annihilator of values, a harsh critic of man as he is.

With the completion of *Zarathustra*, Nietzsche says, "The Yes-saying part of my task had been solved, the turn had come for the No-say, *No-doing* part: the revaluation of our values so far, the great war. . . ." [27] And the major "no" was said to Christianity which, like Judaism before it, was viewed as a "slave" or "herd" morality, the manifestation of the will to power of the lowly, the sick, the rancorous, the impotent.[28] The weak and ignoble overcame themselves and what was noble (such as ancient Rome) by inverting all values, by calling the proud strength of the nobility *evil* and their own impotence *good*. Humility instead of pride, altruism instead of self-affirming egoism— with this corruption, this castration, of the noble man's instinctive values, the slaves came to dominate western man. They, and the priests who are their highest embodiment and their masters, turned man's gaze inward, inflicted upon him a sense of sin, a feeling of guilt; and, by so doing, they conquered.[29]

Nietzsche, who prided himself on his *amor fati*, his love of fate, accepted the necessity of this enslavement and suffering. Now, however, the reign of the priests was drawing to a close. The time had come for a "man of the future" who would deliver mankind from the "lapsed ideal" that is Christianity. This man would be a

great and decisive stroke of midday, who will make the will free once more and restore the earth its aim and man his hope; this anti-Christ and anti-nihilist, conqueror of both God and Unbeing—*one day he must come.* . . .[30]

This, in schematic form, is Nietzsche's philosophy, an interpretation of the past, an analysis of the present, a vision of the future. Its thrust is toward a critique of values, and its foundations rest in a particular view of the nature of human life. It developed over time in both form and content, from a period of discipleship through one of anarchy to one of mastery. Nietzsche himself lived a life of virtual

[27] Nietzsche, *Ecce Homo*, in Kaufmann, ed., *On the Genealogy of Morals and Ecce Homo*, p. 311.

[28] Limitations of space preclude adequate annotation of Nietzsche's argument. I have, however, tried to remain true to the rhetoric of *Beyond Good and Evil* and *The Genealogy of Morals*.

[29] Nietzsche devotes the second and extremely perceptive section of *On the Genealogy of Morals* to the origins of guilt and conscience.

[30] Nietzsche, *The Genealogy of Morals*, in Goffling, ed., *The Birth of Tragedy and The Genealogy of Morals*, p. 230.

isolation, conversing and existing primarily through his written words. These words, however, he viewed as being of enormous importance and power. Because of what he wrote, he considered himself to be a "destiny," the decisive moment in the history of mankind.[31]

In the next section of this chapter we will search for the origins of these qualities in Nietzsche's early life and try to indicate some of the latent meanings of his philosophical constructs. (Needless to say, no total interpretation of the meaning of his philosophy is being attempted.) Then, in the final section, we will construct a more general psychological model of political philosophers and philosophies.

Friedrich Nietzsche's Life

Early Childhood

In *Beyond Good and Evil* Nietzsche remarked that "every great philosophy up to now" had been "the personal confession of its originator, a type of involuntary and unaware memories. . . ."[32] This statement is certainly true of Nietzsche himself, and nowhere more true than in his views of the history of morality; for the conception of morality he puts forth in his later works is, psychologically speaking, a recapitulation and enlargement of his own moral development. In this section, therefore, we shall compare Nietzsche's early life history with his history of morality, bringing both to their natural culmination in the Zarathustrian prophecy.

Nietzsche's father, Karl Ludwig Nietzsche, was a Lutheran clergyman and the son of a clergyman. He was born in 1813, the year of Richard Wagner's birth, and in 1841 became pastor of the town of Röcken, in Prussian Saxony. Earlier he had made the acquaintance of Friedrich Wilhelm IV, whose intervention secured him his position. In 1843 he met Fransziska Oehler, the seventeen-year-old daughter of anther clergyman, and he married her in October of the same year. Their first son was born on October 15, the Kaiser's birthday, in 1844, and was named Friedrich Wilhelm, Fritz for short, in honor of the family's benefactor. Thus, throughout his childhood, Nietzsche's birthday was a national holiday. His sense of his own importance in his maturity probably stems to some small degree from this coincidence.

Karl Nietzsche was a gentle man, a talented amateur musician,

---

[31] See "Why I Am a Destiny," the last chapter of *Ecce Homo*.
[32] Nietzsche, *Beyond Good and Evil* (Chicago: Henry Regnery Co., 1955), p. 6.

and, like his son, was myopic. His daughter Elisabeth, born in 1846, described him as

an extraordinarily sensitive man, or, as was said of him at the time, he took everything so much to heart. Any sign of discord either in the parish or in his own family was so painful to him that he would withdraw to his study and refuse to eat or drink, or speak with anybody.[33]

Nietzsche's father was thus markedly different from either Earl Little or Randolph Churchill. His position in his family was based upon a form of psychic coercion rather than upon the exercise of more typically masculine prerogatives. He would make others feel that any aggressive action on their part would cause him to suffer. Consequently, those who loved him would turn their aggressive feelings inward, so that the inhibited and pent-up aggression would be transformed into feelings of guilt. The parallel between this process and Nietzsche's idea of the slave revolt in morals is evident.

Indeed, Elisabeth reports that Nietzsche was "very hot-tempered" as a child, "a characteristic which he did not like to have mentioned in later years because, in accordance with the family tradition of the Nietzsches, he soon learned to control himself." [34] He was, in other words, very much like his pre-Christian nobles, knowing nothing of good and evil, judging his own actions not by their intent but by their results. A strong conscience, one ensuring Christian behavior, was, however, the "family tradition," a tradition accentuated by the father's use of his own suffering as a technique for punishing others.

Fritz was also his father's favorite, and was, therefore, doubly subject to the ambivalence that characterized the emotional life of the Nietzsche household. What confusion and intrapsychic conflict must have arisen in his mind when, in 1848, his father suffered an accident from which he never fully recovered. Loss of appetite and severe headaches were followed by diminishing mental competence; and, on July 30, 1849, Karl Nietzsche died. He left behind a family consisting of his widow, his mother, two maiden aunts, Fritz, Elisabeth, and a younger son named Joseph.

In studying both Malcolm X and Churchill we found that the loss of their fathers had a profound impact upon their development. The ambivalence and guilt the loss entailed led Malcolm first to rebel against, and then to serve devotedly, other men. These same feelings

[33] Elisabeth Forster-Nietzsche, *The Young Nietzsche* (London: William Heineman, 1912), p. 15. Nietzsche's sister often distorts radically Nietzsche's relations with others, especially his relationship to herself and Lou Salome.

[34] *Ibid.*, p. 12.

led Churchill to identify with his father in order to gain Lord Randolph's power and authority. Nietzsche, as we shall see, tried at various time to identify with his father, to serve him, to live without him, and, finally, to recreate him.

It is not too much to say that with his father's death Nietzsche's period of "nobility" ended, and ended tragically. Karl Nietzsche died at the height of his son's oedipal period, when ambivalence toward the father and sexual longing for the mother are both at their most intense. Also at this age the distinction between word, or thought, and deed is even less clear than it is later. The child still retains a substantial sense of his "omnipotence of thought," the power of his wishes to affect directly the fate of others.[35] Thus, in Nietzsche's unconscious thoughts, his father's death would have been his doing, his "deed." And how powerful were his thoughts, his wishes, his will to power! Powerful enough to have "unchained this earth from its sun," to have killed God.

"He was equal to his deed when he did it; but he could not bear its image after it was done." Like the tragic Greeks and heroic Romans he so admired, Nietzsche's independence and pride were undermined by guilt, by the memory of what he had "done." This image broke through to consciousness in a dream he had soon after his father's death and recorded in an autobiographical sketch written when he was fourteen:

When one despoils a tree of its crown it withers and the birds desert its branches. . . . About this time I had a dream in which I heard mournful organ music, as if at a burial. And as I was trying to discover the cause of this playing, a tomb opened sharply and my father appeared, clad in his shroud. He crossed the church, and returned with a little child in his arms. The tomb opened again, my father disappeared into it, and the stone swung back to its place. At once the wail of the organ ceased, and I awoke. The next morning I told the dream to my dear mother. A short while after, my little brother Joseph fell ill, and after a nervous crisis of a few hours, he died. Our grief was terrible. My dream was exactly fulfilled, for the little body was placed in the arms of its father. After this double calamity the Lord in heaven was our sole consolation.[36]

In *The Interpretation of Dreams* Freud argues that dreams are the fulfillments of unconscious wishes, and that each part of a dream grows out of several impulses and trains of thought. He also cautions that no dream can be fully understood without the associations of

[35] See Freud's discussion of omnipotence of thought in *Totem and Taboo* (*Standard Ed.*, 13), Part III.

[36] Cited in Daniel Halèvy, *Life of Friedrich Nietzsche* (London: T. Fisher Unwin, 1911), p. 21.

the dreamer. Yet there are several things one can say about this dream with some degree of assurance, for many of the themes of Nietzsche's life and thought are epitomized in it.

First, in the dream Nietzsche both brings his father back to life and again consigns him to his grave. In other words, he attempts restitution for the psychic slaying of his father, and then repeats his original action. His ambivalence toward his father thus gives rise to a repetitive cycle of what might be termed criminality and repentance, a cycle not unlike Malcolm's.

As Nietzsche himself interpreted the dream, he also consigned his younger brother to the tomb. Viewed this way, the "double calamity" is a double murder: the remaining male rival for his mother's affection is dispatched. When his brother then actually died, both Nietzsche's feelings of guilt and his unconscious sense of the omnipotence of his thoughts would have been greatly intensified.

There might, however, be an additional meaning to this aspect of the dream; for the child could also have been Nietzsche himself, reunited in the world of the dead with the father he loved. Nietzsche, after all, was his father's favorite child; and throughout his life Nietzsche revered his father's memory. Was his dream perhaps, therefore, a *liebestod*, a vision of a love-death? Was not the music that "overstretch[ed] . . . his soul's pinions" in the third act of Wagner's *Tristan and Isolde* evocative of the organ music in his dream? [37] For the opera also ends in a *liebestod*, a mystical union of Tristan and Isolde in the "world-soul's depths profound." [38] Again we find indications of the intense ambivalences of Nietzsche's personality, as well as of the elements that drew him to Wagner's music during his adolescence.

Finally, after the death of his brother Nietzche states that "the Lord in heaven was [their] sole consolation." As Malcolm X appealed from his god that failed, Elijah Muhammad, to the God in heaven, so young Nietzsche turned his eyes upward. For the next several years he was to be a devoted son of his father's God.

School Days

From the time of his father's death until he was about sixteen, Nietzsche harnessed his "will to power," the masculine and aggressive

[37] Nietzsche, *The Birth of Tragedy,* in Goffling, ed., *The Birth of Tragedy and The Genealogy of Morals,* p. 127.

[38] These lines are part of Isolde's closing aria, in which Nietzsche was later to feel the presence of Schopenhauer's "will" and his Dionysiac spirit.

components of his personality, to priestly and ascetic goals. Latency is, in any case, the time when the first disciplined learning takes place. But where Churchill played intensively with his toy soldiers and Malcolm started to learn to fend for himself, Nietzsche became a moralist like his father.

After Karl Nietzsche's death, the family moved to Naumburg, where Fritz was enrolled in a public school. He appears to have looked down upon his classmates, who were of a lower social rank, and to have inflicted biblical citation upon them rather often. He carried himself so piously, in fact, that, as his sister reports, he won the nickname of "the little Minister." Piety and righteousness, however, are not terribly endearing to preadolescent boys; and Fritz seems to have been virtually friendless at this school. He was, therefore, soon transferred to private schools, which he found more congenial and where he made a few friends.

Fritz was known to his friends for his melancholy, studiousness, and piety. One of them observed that he "had an exceedingly pious and deep soul" and that "from his earliest youth he began preparing himself for the calling which he then wished to adopt—that of the Church." [39] His sister even records that an "otherwise very rationalistic law student" said "Fritz reminded him of the twelve-year-old Jesus," but this story may be apocryphal.[40] At the same time, however, Fritz played imaginary games, put on well-planned theatrical performances for the family, and avidly followed the course of the Crimean War. Yet even his recreational activity was mental rather than physical, a matter of words rather than of deeds. Churchill and Malcolm X, by contrast, were much involved in physical activity at this age.

By the time he was ten years old, young Nietzsche was also starting to write poetry and compose music. The latter activity was inspired by an Ascension Day performance of Handel's *Messiah*. The "Hallelujah Chorus" sounded to him like "the angels' song of rejoicing" as Jesus ascended to heaven, and he immediately set about to write something like it.[41] One would guess that he felt his father's beatification in the music, and sought similarly to praise him.

After his initial difficulties at school, Fritz soon became the best student in his class. This fact, too, fed his sense of being somehow different, and somehow superior. When he was thirteen, both he and

[39] Quoted in Forster-Nietzsche, *op. cit.*, p. 42.
[40] *Ibid.*, p. 43.
[41] *Ibid.*, p. 56.

Elisabeth drew special attention from the school inspectors for the excellence of their work. In her biography of her brother, Elisabeth describes the conversation they had about the incident:

When he and I were alone that afternoon, however, he said to me: "Isn't it funny that both of us learn so well and know so many things that other children don't know?" After we had discussed the matter for a little while the secret motive for his last question became apparent. "I always wonder," he said in a low voice, "whether it is not possible that our dear Papa in heaven is the cause of it, and whether he does not give us our good thoughts. . . ." [42]

Assuming the essential veracity of this report, we would surmise that young Nietzsche felt he had a special relationship with his dead, but somehow still omnipotent, father.[43] In ascribing his school success to his father, he was transforming his feeling of loss into one of gain: "I am not unusually deprived," he is saying. "Rather I am unusually blessed." At the same time, he seems to be viewing himself in large part as the passive agent of his father's power. He is thereby disclaiming any credit, and also any blame, for his actions.

Unconsciously, to go one step farther, Nietzsche probably feared his father's power, or rather the attacks of his conscience. In order to ward off punishment and to continue being successful at school, he became a young parson, the inheritor of his father's role. He served, in other words, his Father(s) in heaven as did his father before him.

There was, however, an unresolved ambivalence here; for Nietzsche had assumed for himself active and passive roles which might well come into conflict with each other. For by emulating his father, he was also challenging him, just as imitation of God is a sacrilege. The result of such an assault could only be castration or, perhaps, his father's fate ("I am already dead as my father . . ."). Accepting the passive role, the role of his father's instrument, would ensure his survival ("while as my mother I am still living and becoming old"); but it would also condemn him to subservience and impotency. During latency, when the basic drives are less pressing than during the genital phase or adolescence, Nietzsche could maintain an intrapsychic balance by devoting himself fiercely to a Christian vocation. Such a balance could not, however, be maintained indefinitely.

The first marked signs of intrapsychic conflict came in 1886–1887, when Nietzsche started to suffer from the eye trouble and headaches

[42] *Ibid.*, p. 63.

[43] Unconsciously, we never fully accept death; there is always some residual belief that a deceased person is just away and will someday return.

that were to plague him all of his life.[44] These may have resulted in part from the physiological weakness of his eyes, which he inherited from his father, or from an unconscious desire to escape the tensions of academic competition by making school work impossible. One would also guess that Nietzsche was starting to identify with his father's weaknesses as well as his strengths, that the psychic strain of balancing his assertive and submissive impulses was being manifested physically in the same symptoms Karl Nietzsche had just before his death.

As long as Nietzsche continued to live at home, he was able to use his Christian faith to hold his conflicting impulses in check. But in 1859, when he was fourteen, his academic achievement won him admission to the Royal School in Pforta, a well-known and rigorous Lutheran institution.[45] He was homesick and friendless during his first year at this genuinely ascetic school, where body, soul, and almost all waking hours were committed to learning and God. By his second year, however, a yearning for knowledge came upon him, a sign that his family's reverence for God was starting to be undermined by a competing world view. He now had, in his own words, an "inward desire for universal culture," a desire still grounded in "religion, the foundation of all knowledge." [46] As in his first musical compositions, Nietzsche's efforts were not lacking in grandiosity. As both earlier and later, he needed to comprehend everything in order to provide his conscious mind with adequate defenses against his own impulses. As we shall see, in the short run "universal culture" was not the guarantor of psychic balance that his father's religion had been.

As Nietzsche's devotion to culture increased, his commitment to religion declined. One precipitant of this change may have been the death of his maternal grandfather during his second year at Pforta. With his death, the last family representative of God passed from the scene. And, strangely enough, the summer before his grandfather died Nietzsche dreamed that "he had seen [his grandfather's parsonage] lying in ruins, and [his] . . . grandmother sitting alone beneath its shattered framework amid the debris." [47] Thus the young man was once again the prophet of doom, the "pale criminal."

The final blows to Nietzsche's faith seem, however, to have been the

---

[44] Forster-Nietzsche, *op. cit.,* p. 63.

[45] It was just before he entered the Royal School that Nietzsche wrote the precocious autobiography mentioned earlier. The amount of writing Nietzsche did during his childhood and adolescence is rather phenomenal.

[46] Quoted from Nietzsche's diary, October 25, 1859, in Forster-Nietzsche, *op. cit.,* p. 85.

[47] *Ibid.,* p. 87.

failure of confirmation to reveal any great transfiguring secret,[48] and the reading of David Strauss's *The Life of Jesus*, which was a major attack upon the historical veracity of the Bible story.[49] But without faith, "Are we not plunging continually? . . . Is there any up or down left? . . . Has it not become colder?" And "How shall we, the murderers of all murderers, comfort ourselves?"

During his last few years at Pforta, Nietzsche's work declined somewhat as the inner turmoil of loss of faith began to take its toll. He also showed some signs of the modest adolescent rebellion that dominated his first year at college; but, as a note he made in the spring of 1862 shows, it was the "death of God" that dominated his mind:

How often have I not thought that all our philosophy is like the Tower of Babel; to storm the heavens is the aim of all great aspirations. . . . An infinite confusion of ideas among the people is the discomforting result. . . . I have attempted to deny everything: Oh! destruction is easy, but construction! [50]

Nietzsche did not yet have anything to replace God, to replace his father, nor would he until he discovered Schopenhauer and Wagner.

Thus far Nietzsche's experience parallels rather exactly his history of morals. The early heroic period ends, with the death of his father, in tragedy and the birth of guilt. Then follows a long phase of ascetic devotion to his father's God, which terminates in the death of God during his adolescence. In his later writings Nietzsche accuses Christianity (rather than his father) of being castrative, of bringing to an end the rule of the nobles. The priests, by making men feel guilty, deprived them of their freedom and masculinity. In order for men to release their energies, to express their will to power, it then became necessary for them to devote themselves to spiritualized or sublimated activities, to moral activities. From this ascetic devotion comes, however, the growth of the human spirit:

All this tyranny, this arbitrariness, this rigorous and grandiose stupidity has *disciplined* and *educated* the spirit.[51]

In his theory of moral evolution Nietzsche thus seems to be describing his own development, explaining and justifying it to himself and

[48] Nietzsche was confirmed with his friend Paul Deussen, whose account of their mutual disillusionment is quoted in Forster-Nietzsche, *op. cit.,* p. 89.

[49] *Ibid.,* p. 90. David Strauss, it should be remembered, is the same man Nietzsche accused of being the arch-Philistine in his *Untimely Meditations.* Having used Strauss to attack his father's beliefs, he now attacked Strauss in defending his surrogate father, Richard Wagner.

[50] *Ibid.*

[51] Nietzsche, *Beyond Good and Evil,* p. 96.

to others. The impotency of his school days, his subservience to religious ideals, was not his responsibility or his weakness. Rather, twenty centuries of Christian belief imposed upon him the "ghastly paradox of a crucified god, the unspeakably cruel mystery of God's self-crucifixion for the benefit of mankind." [52] The image of his suffering father is in this way covered over with the image of God on the cross; the guilt and self-torment of his very individual murderous "deed" is disguised behind the more general idea of Christian guilt and sin. At the same time this suffering was necessary for Nietzsche's own growth, for his own progress toward spiritual freedom . . . one must, after all, love one's fate (*amor fati*).

One might hypothesize, therefore, that one of the purposes of any historical theory, for its originator or those who adhere to it, is to make comprehensible and morally acceptable the person's own past. In this respect, the Black Muslim creed and Nietzsche's philosophy perform a similar function. And, like the Black Muslim doctrine, Nietzsche's philosophy also provides an enemy for the present and a hope for the future.

Nietzsche as Disciple

What might be termed the second cycle, the second instance of the recurrent pattern of Nietzsche's life, began just after his graduation from Pforta. A leisurely trip down the Rhine was followed by his enrollment in the University of Bonn, and his joining of the Franconia fraternity.

In the past Nietzsche had shunned large groups and boisterous activity. His participation in the activities of a fraternity, one of many of its kind dedicated to drinking, singing, fencing, and women, thus signified an attempt to change direction. Characteristically, he was uneasy about his decision; projecting his own uncertainty and censoriousness onto his family, he wrote:

Now, I can see with my mind's eye how you people are shaking your heads in a most peculiar manner, giving forth with a cry of astonishment. There are, indeed, many wonderful things connected with this step and, therefore, I shall not blame you.[53]

He then goes on to create a picture, which was soon proved to be a false one, of how high-minded and congenial Franconia would be.

---

[52] Nietzsche, *The Genealogy of Morals*, in Goffling, ed., *The Birth of Tragedy and The Genealogy of Morals*, p. 169.

[53] Karl F. Leidecker, ed., *Nietzsche: Unpublished Letters* (London: Peter Owen, 1959), p. 29. From a letter dated October 24 and 25, 1864.

Nonetheless, Nietzsche spent the academic year dutifully liberating himself from duty. He tried hard to enjoy himself, without quite succeeding. As he wrote home:

I am frequently unhappy, . . . I have too many moods and am rather inclined to be a nagging spirit, not only to myself but also to others.[54]

Nietzsche had, however, no ready alternative to the life he was leading. Neither philology nor theology provided much comfort or stimulation. Indeed, he commented that philology, the careful, scientific study of ancient texts, was emasculating:

I set great store by self-development, [he wrote to a friend] but how easily one can be rendered impotent by men like Ritschl and be carried away into channels which are, perhaps, far removed from one's own inclinations.[55]

Ritschl was one of the leading philologists in Germany and soon was to become Nietzsche's guide. At this juncture he seemed to be only a threat to the young man's intellectual independence. Or, to put it another way, Nietzsche was already casting Ritschl in the role of a substitute father, who demanded of his "son" dutiful attention to matters "far removed from one's own inclinations." Impotence would result from complying with the father's wishes, as it had in the past; but the threat of castration, of emasculating guilt, hung over all efforts to abandon priestly activities. For Nietzsche even the normal activities of a college freshman constituted a fearful rebellion against his father's dictates. Nietzsche bore the burden of this guilt for a year, and may even have visited a prostitute once or twice; [56] at the end of the year, in his own words, he "left Bonn like a fugitive." [57]

Thus ended the rebellious, "heroic" moment in this phase of Nietzsche's life. He decided to start his academic career over at the University of Leipzig, where Ritschl had also gone to escape certain controversies that had arisen in Bonn. He was determined to lead a more disciplined life, although he was not sure to what end. It was in this mood that he discovered Schopenhauer's redeeming pessimism:

At that time [1865] I stood absolutely alone, full of the most painful experiences and disappointments, without either help, fundamental prin-

---

[54] Quoted in Forster-Nietzsche, *op. cit.,* p. 133.

[55] Leidecker, *op. cit.,* p. 4. From a letter dated August 30, 1865.

[56] Nietzsche's madness was presumably of syphilitic origin; if so, he would have picked up the infection during his year at Bonn.

[57] Quoted in Forster-Nietzsche, *op. cit.,* p. 146.

ciples, hopes, or even pleasant memories. . . . One day I came across [*The World as Will and Idea*] at old Rohn's curiosity shop. . . . I know not what demon whispered to me: "Take this book home with thee." . . . In this book, in which every line cried out renunciation, denial, and resignation, I saw a mirror in which I espied the whole world, life and my own mind depicted in frightful grandeur. . . . here I saw illness and recovery, banishment and refuge, hell and heaven.[58]

Nietzsche, like Malcolm X when he discovered Elijah Muhammad, was in need of a faith, one that would explain to him his own condition and relieve him of all individual responsibility for that condition. In Schopenhauer Nietzsche read that the world itself was dominated by an irrational will to life, that asceticism and art were the only ways to survive in it. Here, then, was the familiar call to the priestly life, here was a new God and father to serve. As Nietzsche wrote in the *Untimely Meditation* on Schopenhauer:

Schopenhauer speaks to himself, and if one wants to imagine a listener, let him think of a son whom his father is instructing.[59]

Schopenhauer thus gave Nietzsche a vision of himself filled with "frightful grandeur." In order to realize it, Nietzsche set about determinedly to do penance for his sins, to be fully ascetic and thereby kill the "will to life" that deprived man of serenity:

By drawing all my qualities and my aspirations before the forum of gloomy self-contempt I became bitter, unjust, and unbridled in my hatred of myself. I even practiced bodily penance; for instance, I forced myself for a fortnight at a stretch to go to bed at 2 o'clock in the morning and to rise punctually at six.[60]

In this manner Nietzsche sought to control his adolescent sexuality and aggressiveness. He avoided almost all proximity to women—except Ritschl's motherly wife—and did not permit himself to enjoy the academic successes that were starting to come his way.

Under Ritschl's kindly guidance, Nietzsche rapidly developed the reputation of being the most promising young philologist at Leipzig. So good was his work, in fact, that in 1869 he was offered a professorship at the University of Basel, before he had even completed his doctorate. The formalities were waived; and, at the age of twenty-five, Nietzsche seemed well on his way to a brilliant academic career.

[58] *Ibid.*, p. 152.
[59] Friedrich Nietzsche, *Schopenhauer as Educator* (Chicago: Henry Regnery Co., 1965), p. 13.
[60] Quoted in Forster-Nietzsche, *op. cit.*, p. 153.

Shortly after his arrival at Basel, Nietzsche added a new god to his pantheon. Before leaving Leipzig he had met Richard Wagner, whose music he had long loved. He was immediately captivated by the man and his fascinating wife Cosima. The Wagners, he discovered, were living at Tribschen, not far from Basel, and they invited the young admirer to visit them. Nietzsche did so, and soon became an ancillary member of the household. He basked in the praise of this man he so much admired, and gave praise fulsomely in return. He wrote, for instance, to a friend that Wagner

is ruled by such an absolute kind of ideality, by such profound and touching humanity, and by such a lofty and serious interest in life, that by his side I feel in the presence of the divine.[61]

Nietzsche was, in other words, a loyal disciple and a worshipful son to this man who was born in the same year as his father, who also professed to honor Schopenhauer, and whose music gave him such emotional release.

Cosima Wagner exercised just as great an attraction for Nietzsche as did her husband. That the attraction was sexual is clearly and sadly shown by the telegram Nietzsche sent Cosima as he was going mad ("Ariadne, I love you. Dionysus.") and by his statement, made after his confinement, that "My wife Cosima Wagner brought me hither." [62] This latter statement also indicates that, probably unconsciously at the time and with increasing consciousness as the years passed, Nietzsche identified himself with Wagner. In short, he created a complete and striking oedipal configuration for himself. From 1869 through 1872, as long as the Wagners lived in Tribschen and provided him with a replacement for the family life he had never fully enjoyed, Nietzsche seemed content to play the son's role. Tribschen was for him an "Isle of the Blessed," a metaphor he later attached to one of the stopping points along Zarathustra's journey.

Nietzsche's work at this time was an attempt to serve all three of his gods. Thus *The Birth of Tragedy* grew out of his philological researches, was cast in Schopenhauerian language, and lauded Wagner's operas as a new union of the Apollonian and Dionysiac forces. His ambivalence toward his own half-scholarly, half-musical position is shown by his attack on Socratism, on the one hand, and his new ideal of the "music-practicing Socrates," on the other; for surely Nietzsche

[61] *Ibid.*, p. 214.

[62] The most extensive discussion of Nietzsche's madness is B. F. Podach, *The Madness of Nietzsche* (London: Putnam, 1931).

wished to fill that role himself, and to gain with it a harmonious, dynamic union of reason and passion.

The Birth of Tragedy won a most unfavorable reception from Nietzsche's fellow scholars, a fact that did nothing to lessen the pointedness of Nietzsche's attack on German culture in the first two of the *Untimely Meditations*. The essays on Schopenhauer and Wagner were manifestly of a different character, words of praise rather than assaults. In fact, however, they were Nietzsche's final efforts to remain true to dying gods. And Nietzsche "kills" each man by transforming him from a human being into an archetype. Schopenhauer becomes the ideal philosopher; Wagner, the ideal artist. Nietzsche later recognized that this deification was, in his own words, "an assassination." [63]

Nietzsche had been "overcoming" his devotion to Wagner and Schopenhauer for some time. The break with Wagner had been developing since the composer left Tribschen for Bayreuth in 1872. Although Nietzsche continued to be welcome among the Wagnerians, he was no longer the favorite son. Thus, with his health rapidly declining, Nietzsche left the first Bayreuth festival in 1876. Wagner turned Philistine, and, in *Parsifal*, Wagner turned religious. In short, Wagner betrayed Nietzsche in order to gain the applause of exactly those people Nietzsche had himself abandoned. Nietzsche might well have said of Wagner what Malcolm said of Elijah Muhammad, "I believed in him more than he believed in himself." That Wagner also told Nietzsche's doctor that he attributed the younger man's ill-health to excessive masturbation [64] undoubtedly helped to confirm Nietzsche's view that this *ersatz* father-son relationship should be ended.

Nietzsche as Prophet

The break with Wagner marks the beginning of the next cycle of Nietzsche's life. Once again Nietzsche had heroically broken with his father; once again he was his own man. The consequences were a profound uneasiness and great physical misery. *Human, All-Too-Human*, in its increasingly fragmentary style from the first part through *The Wanderer and His Shadow*, parallels the shattering of Nietzsche's bodily intactness. The physical symptoms that accompanied his father's decline—gastric disorders, headaches, and loss of vision—were now more than ever Nietzsche's own.

Nietzsche was, in fact, approaching the age (thirty-six) at which

[63] Nietzsche, *Ecce Homo,* in Kaufmann, ed., *On the Genealogy of Morals and Ecce Homo,* p. 277.

[64] Robert W. Gutman, *Richard Wagner* (New York: Harcourt, Brace and World, Inc., 1968), p. 360.

his father had died, at which Nietzsche had "killed" him. He had, moreover, destroyed Wagner's paternity over him. "God is dead. God remains dead." Would not his rebellious but loving son die with him? Nietzsche's guilt, in other words, the repressive force of his conscience, transformed his striving for aggressive and sexual release into an hysterical identification with his father.[65]

With the passing of the year of his father's death, Nietzsche's health became less critical and his spirits improved. Then, in August, 1881, he conceived the idea of eternal recurrence in one of the ecstatic moods that accompanied his creative periods throughout the 1880's.

In several ways, 1881 was different from the previous years of Nietzsche's life. Before this time, his feelings of guilt and ill-health had led him to sever his ties with almost everyone he knew. He had become a lonesome wanderer, seeking respite in motion and change of location. Now, alone, he had faced what he believed to be the appointed hour of his doom and survived. Even the spell of Wagnerian music was at last broken, as "the phoenix of music flew past us with lighter and more brilliant feathers than it had ever displayed before." [66] And he had found, in Sils-Maria in the upper Engadine, a new, quiet, and lofty spot from which to survey the condition of his fellowmen. With his health somewhat better, he felt reborn and had the courage to ask himself: "This life, as thou livest it at present, and hast lived it, thou must live it once more. . . . Dost thou want this once more, and also for innumerable times?" [67]

Nietzsche answered affirmatively, an affirmation that grew out of, or grew into, a mood of absolute euphoria. He wrote to one of his few remaining close friends:

The intensity of my emotions makes me shudder and laugh. A few times I felt unable to leave my room for the ridiculous reason that my eyes were inflamed. And why? I had wept too much on my wanderings the day before; not sentimental tears, but tears of jubilation, tears mingled with song and nonsensical chatter; my soul was filled with a new vision.[68]

The distinction between joy and sorrow, sense and nonsense, speech and song had been obliterated. Nietzsche felt the mood that he was to immortalize in the dithyrambs with which he concluded the third

[65] On hysteria, see Otto Fenichel, *The Psychoanalytic Theory of Neurosis* (New York: W. W. Norton and Company, Inc., 1945), Chap. 12.

[66] Nietzesche, *Ecce Homo*, in Kaufmann, ed., *On the Genealogy of Morals and Ecce Homo*, p. 295.

[67] Nietzsche, *The Gay Science*, in Kaufmann, ed., *The Portable Nietzsche*, p. 271.

[68] Quoted in the editor's introduction to *The Gay Science*, p. 2.

book of *Zarathustra*. These "seven seals," as Nietzsche called them, have as their refrain:

> Oh, how should I not lust after eternity
> and after the nuptial ring of rings, the
> ring of recurrence?
>   Never yet have I found the woman from
> whom I wanted children, unless it be this
> woman whom I love: for I love you, O eternity.
> *For I love you, O eternity!* [69]

Eternal recurrence, then, is more a feeling than an idea, an ecstasy of primal love, a merging of all pain and pleasure into a climactic joy. Feeling himself freed from the obligation to serve ascetically the fathers, the gods, the idols of this world, Nietzsche experienced a sublimated lover's ecstasy. In that supreme experience all the suffering of his life was justified.

Yet it was in words and not in deeds that Nietzsche's love was consummated. Just as he had killed his father in phantasy only, so his victory was only in the realm of pure feeling. When he tried to translate this vision into experience, in his short-lived courtship of Lou Salome, he found that all the grandeur of his ideas, all his veneration for what was eternal and feminine, could not win him the love of a woman of flesh and blood. And this failure almost destroyed his newfound ability to affirm. He took "a tremendous dose of opium" and weathered the crisis. On Christmas Day, 1882, he wrote to a friend, describing the affair with Lou: "This last *morsel of life* was the hardest I have chewed thus far and it is still possible I will *choke* on it." [70] In *Zarathustra* it is the great nausea that is the final challenge Zarathustra must meet on his way to the affirmation of the "seven seals"; and it is a shepherd choking on a snake that symbolizes this danger.

Before the "sudden birth" of *Zarathustra*, eternal recurrence was a sterile principle. It did not bring Nietzsche success in love, nor by itself did it generate further work. Not until the idea of the will to power was joined to it did Nietzsche again become productive.

In February, 1883, Nietzsche experienced once again the ecstasy of eternal recurrence. This time, however, he translated the feelings directly into written work; or, in his own terms, he accepted "inspiration." He felt himself to be "merely incarnation, merely mouthpiece,

---

[69] Nietzsche, *Thus Spoke Zarathustra*, in Kaufmann, ed., *The Portable Nietzsche*, p. 340.

[70] Leidecker, *op. cit.*, p. 97. From a letter to Franz Overbeck.

merely a medium of overpowering forces." [71] He thus accepted a feminine, a passive, position. In order to give birth to Zarathustra, in order to bring forth Zarathustra out of the womb of eternal recurrence, he had to become the "medium of overpowering forces." In other words, the creation of *Zarathustra* was, for Nietzsche, the experiencing of the powerful masculine, impregnating force which he called the will to power. In accepting the will to power as the complement to eternal recurrence, Nietzsche had created the metaphysical unity out of which a new god could be born.

It might also be mentioned that *Zarathustra* is clearly intended as a modern tragedy, the rebirth of tragedy that Wagnerian opera promised but did not realize. Zarathustra the dancer and the celebrator of life would reveal the emptiness of Parsifal's ascetic quest for the Holy Grail. No wonder Nietzsche was struck by the fact that Wagner died just as Zarathustra was born—inescapably Nietzsche's fate was that of the pale criminal.

Nietzsche succeeded in transforming the fundamental problem of his emotional life into a philosophical system. All masculine striving, both sexual and aggressive, was reduced to the will to power. All feminine receptivity was embodied in eternal recurrence. Yet the union was not perfect, not eternal, just as the ecstasies out of which it grew passed and left the familiar illnesses and depressions in their wake. To guard against his own frailty, and to provide himself with a justification for continuing his attack upon the old gods, Nietzsche created the *übermensch*, a man-god of self-overcoming.

Until his madness descended fully upon him, Nietzsche never confused himself with the *übermensch*. Nietzsche-Zarathustra was rather a bridge to this new form of divine humanity. But to prepare man for this destiny, to help him overcome the human, all-too-human, it was necessary to annihilate old gods, destroy old idols; therefore, Zarathustra was at once a yea-sayer and a nay-sayer, an affirmer of the future and a transformer of the past.

In serving the *übermensch*, Nietzsche was attempting to resolve the ambivalence that still plagued him, to establish for himself a position in which he could dutifully obey the god he had himself created. He gave birth to a deity, and then became its prophet. Yet Nietzsche in the role of prophet is itself a paradox, as he himself realized. For this reason Zarathustra cautions his disciples to be ashamed of Zarathustra, to watch out for his deceptions. Nietzsche knew only too well himself the dangers of faith, the vengeance and waywardness of all

[71] Nietzsche, *Ecce Homo,* in Kaufmann, ed., *On the Genealogy of Morals and Ecce Homo,* p. 300.

gods. He could not, therefore, even have faith in the man-god he had created; for the prophet of the will to power was perpetually in doubt, perpetually lacking the will to transform thought into deed. As he wrote to the philosopher Brandes late in his life, "I myself rarely display the valor to acknowledge what I really know." [72] Ultimately, Nietzsche lacked the power to stand alone, to speak for his ideas as Churchill spoke for England. Hence he covered his doubts and impotency in overstatement, his ambivalences in bold paradoxes. He bravely says "yes!" and "no!"; but one senses that he feels "maybe."

The "maybe" was finally resolved into the manic state of late 1888, which produced his last works and culminated in his madness. Then, at last, Nietzsche's stretched and overstretched mind ceased to work. In his final ecstatic moments he wrote to Peter Gast that "the world is transfigured and all the heavens are glad," and signed his note "The Crucified One." To others he signed himself "Dionysus." And he wrote to Jacob Burckhart, "What is inconvenient and hurts my modesty is that ultimately every name in history is I." [73] The antipodes of Nietzsche's personality had at last been resolved—into the unity of psychosis.

Philosophers and Philosophies

Philosophers, like leaders and adherents, are political men. Nietzsche, no less than the other men, displaced private emotions, most importantly of an aggressive nature, onto public objects and rationalized them in terms of a public interest. Nietzsche never attacked his father, or his father's memory; rather he displaced his ambivalent feelings from the familial context into the public arena, and constructed around them a web of beliefs which helped him to ward off the incursions of his own impulses on the one hand, and his feelings of guilt on the other. More precisely, he developed over the years successive sets of beliefs, each of which challenged accepted authority and argued for a change in values. Eventually, with his acceptance of the will to power, Nietzsche thought he had discovered the dynamus of all such change.

In his reliance upon displacement, and his concern for power and authority, Nietzsche is similar to Malcolm X and Churchill. He resembles Malcolm, moreover, in that he lives out a cyclical pattern of rebellion and submission; and he is like Churchill in that he ultimately

---

[72] Leidecker, *op. cit.,* p. 125. From a letter dated December 2, 1887.
[73] *Ibid.,* pp. 154–155.

finds the superior power and authority of any other man intolerable. There is, in other words, adherency and leadership in political theory as well as in political practice. For both philosophers and activists, it is the nature of the relationship with the father that seems to determine whether the leader's or the follower's role will be played.

There are, however, a number of ways in which philosophers differ from political activists. Nietzsche was, for example, as much a warrior as was Churchill; but war for him was a matter of words, not of deeds. He shunned the company of other men and delivered his hammer blows from the secure isolation of the Engadine. Theorists, in other words, attach the same potency and importance to their thoughts that activists do to their actions. We might hypothesize that, like Nietzsche, they even feel there is something magical or omnipotent about their verbal formulations, that words are somehow equivalent to deeds. If this view is correct, then part of the attraction of philosophy —which we tend to regard as the most sublimated, the least instinctual, of men's activities—lies in the gratification it provides for the most primitive and infantile of our psychic needs. And, holding this view, we are not surprised that Nietzsche's most sublime moments came when his words expanded to encompass all of existence within themselves, when through his experiencing of eternal recurrence Nietzsche made the cosmos coterminous with his own personality. We are not surprised, that is, that a childlike ecstasy, a feeling of primal unity, was one of the goals of his philosophy.

Put another way, the ultimate goal of the philosopher's life, perhaps of all our lives, is the elimination of psychic conflict. In some sense, of course, tranquility is inevitable; for all men are born to die. Short of physical death, ecstasy and orgasm, madness and sleep, promise us freedom from psychic conflict, absolution from responsibility and choice. Until the final ecstasy of his madness overtook him, Nietzsche tested his ideas against the limits of this absolute experience without mistaking a temporary cessation of conflict for a permanent elimination of the human, all-too-human. He honored, as few men have honored, what is most ecstatic and what is most analytic in human experience. And he suffered as few philosophers have suffered.

To speak more psychoanalytically, one of the functions of political theories is to achieve a balance between the release of emotion and its control. Depending upon the needs of the creator or follower of a theory, this balance will vary. Some theories, like those most commonly turned into political ideologies, define strictly the permissive areas of aggressive (and often sexual) activity. Others, like Nietzsche's, give their believers the chance to express and consummate virtually all of their desires, but with two important limitations. First, the consummation is entirely verbal; second, the logic of paradox, the necessity to affirm and deny, must be obeyed. Thus Nietzsche's theory represents the extreme case of a vehicle for the full expression of ambivalent feeling, while something like the Black Muslim creed permits only a controlled, but a relatively active, consummation of the basic drives.

Political theories, in addition to providing guidance for the expression of feeling and the channeling of drives, also help to explain and justify the individual's life experience. Frequently a model of historical change, one involving moral evolution, is the medium for these functions. Nietzsche, as we have seen, was able to rationalize his suffering by viewing it as an instance of the more general phenomenon of Christian guilt and asceticism. Less consciously, he created a model of historical change that closely paralleled his own psychological development.

Even more obviously, changes in the form and content of a man's philosophy result from alterations in his life circumstances and their attendant emotional needs. Thus we were able to trace the growth of Nietzsche's philosophy, from its original Schopenhauerian form to its culmination in his creation of a new tragic vision, by examining the changes in his personal relations and style of living as the years passed. Here it might be noted that one often distorts the contribution of a political thinker by assuming that all of his ideas must somehow be logically compatible. Our orientation would lead us to believe that all of a man's ideas will be related to each other; but the relationship may be more developmental and emotional than logical.

Three final points may be made about the life history of the political philosopher. First, unlike political leaders and adherents, philosophers show an inclination for intellectual work from an early age. When Churchill was an aspiring soldier, carefully arranging his toy soldiers and leading his younger relatives into battle, Nietzsche was a young priest and scholar. Or, to put it another way, during latency, activists and thinkers both tend to develop, in embryonic form, the skills appropriate to their differing adult vocations.

Second, it is not simply differential ability which leads a man, or a boy, in an activist or philosophical direction. We would hypothesize, rather, that the young philosopher, everything else being equal, is less able to resolve his ambivalences and reduce his feelings of guilt than is the potential activist. Thoughtfulness and doubt, self-consciousness and anxiety are, after all, opposite sides of the same coins.

Finally, political philosophers seem to have a larger feminine component in their personalities than do activists. The activist plays the role of father or son or both. The theorist, in addition, gives birth to his ideas, mothers and nurtures them. In Nietzsche's case, the virtually all-female environment of his early life undoubtedly accentuated his disposition to develop feminine identifications. There are, of course, alternative ways in which the same result might be reached; but the ubiquity of birth metaphors in philosophy indicates the importance of this feminine component.

5

Conclusion

The preceding chapters have been devoted to thinking psychoan-alytically about human nature in politics. By using psychoanalytic theory we were able to find connections among the various life experiences of each man which were not discernible on the manifest level. In each case we found that political activity served as a vehicle for managing the guilt that accompanied the father-son relationship. For Churchill an identification with his father formed the psychological basis for his capacity to lead. Malcolm X's adherency to Elijah Muhammad and the Nation of Islam grew out of his need to be a loyal son to his father. Nietzsche's philosophical activity allowed him to express his highly ambivalent feelings for the father he manifestly loved.

Each of the men is, of course, far more complicated than either this formulaic summary or even our more detailed hypotheses indicate. Many themes in their lives were left untouched in order to accentuate the line of psychological development that culminated most centrally in their political activity. The risk involved in such simplification is that the reader will not gain a sufficient feeling for the man's whole personality. If, however, one also reads the primary sources used here, then this book would serve as a guide for more detailed explorations and study. Alternatively the hypotheses developed about leaders, adherents, and philosophers can be used as starting points for the psychological examination of the lives of other political men.

If the reader decides to go further with this approach, he will discover that using psychoanalytic theory involves joining two not entirely compatible qualities.[1] On the one hand, a feeling for the person-

[1] See the Georges' discussion of this point in the introduction to the Dover paperback edition of their *Woodrow Wilson and Colonel House.*

ality of the man being studied is absolutely essential. One must be able to identify with one's protagonist, to feel what he has felt. Failure to do so will result in a dried-out, dehumanized construct or model, the ashes rather than the essence of the man. Yet there must also be a control over feeling, a theoretical detachment which helps one to avoid confusing the person being studied with the person studying him. One does not, after all, want to suffer Nietzsche's hurt modesty in discovering that "every name in history is I."

In doing work of this kind, one must also be sensitive to the broader social and historical context within which any life is lived. The fact that Churchill was an English aristocrat, that Malcolm X was an American black man, and that Nietzsche was a nineteenth-century German bourgeois affected greatly each of their public lives. Ignoring such factors results in a psychological reductionism which obscures as much as it clarifies.

There is, in fact, an arrogance in assuming that any one theoretical perspective will allow an investigator to gain a complete understanding of a man's personality. Man is by nature multifaceted, and our understanding of him must be the same. Psychoanalysis is, in this regard, attractive just because it accentuates sides of human experience often ignored or even willfully denied. At the same time, it has its limitations. It cannot, for example, explain what determines the greatness of the men we have studied. With it we gain a richer understanding of what is human, all-too-human about these men; we also gain some idea of what predisposes men to political activity and thought. But the excellence of Nietzsche's philosophic artistry or the unusually hypnotic quality of Malcolm's oratory are not explainable psychoanalytically—nor, I suspect, in any other way.

Despite the ambiguities and difficulties involved, despite the residue of what cannot be explained, it is worthwhile to continue studying human nature in politics. Our understanding of the political process cannot be adequate if it is grounded in misunderstandings about man himself. Nor can we make sensible moral judgments, about political men or about ourselves, without being aware of our own mental character. Indeed, one of the advantages of psychoanalytic theory is that it forces us to recognize that there is something political in each of us and personal motivations in every political action. We are all human, all-too-human, and, at least in our dreams and phantasies, we are all heroes and philosopher-kings as well. Perhaps the ultimate justification for psychoanalytic study is that it results in, as Bob Dylan says, "bringing it all back home."

Finally, it should once again be emphasized that the goal of this study has been explanation, not evaluation. Moral judgments should grow out of the study of men's lives, as Plutarch and all other self-conscious biographers have recognized; but empirical analysis of men's lives should be one thing, the moral evaluation of them, another.

Guide to Further Reading

The books most directly bearing upon this study, and the ones out of which it grew, have been cited in the footnotes to each chapter. Here mention will be made of other works which serve to broaden the reader's familiarity with applied psychoanalysis. But once again— the best way to learn about this kind of work is to immerse oneself in psychoanalytic theory and men's lives.

General. There are several classics of applied psychoanalysis that provide philosophic overviews of the field. Norman O. Brown, in *Life Against Death* (New York: Vintage Books, 1959), challenges the assumptions of psychoanalytic thought and attempts to extend its reasoning to new areas. Herbert Marcuse, in *Eros and Civilization* (New York: Vintage Books, 1962), emphasizes the dialectical style of thought which is, to some extent, common to Freud, Marx, and Hegel. Phillip Rieff's *Freud: The Mind of the Moralist* (Garden City, N.Y.: Doubleday & Co., 1961) is probably the best philosophical evaluation of Freud's own achievements. Paul Roazen, in *Freud: Political and Social Thought* (New York: Alfred A. Knopf, 1968), highlights the political implications of Freud's work. The methodological status of applied psychoanalysis, and of personality and politics studies in general, is explored in Fred I. Greenstein, ed., *Personality and Politics*, which is Volume XXIV, No. 3 (July, 1968) of *The Journal of Social Issues*.

The best introduction to applied psychoanalysis is, of course, Freud's work. *Civilization and Its Discontents*, *Future of an Illusion*, and *Leonardo da Vinci* are, next to the works cited in the text, the best starting points. And no reader should deny himself the pleasure and stimulation of *The Interpretation of Dreams*. (All of Freud's works are available in the *Standard Edition*).

Leaders. Here, as indicated earlier, the works of Harold Lasswell are most important. *Psychopathology and Politics* (New York: The

102

Viking Press, 1960) and *Power and Personality* (New York: The Viking Press, 1962) develop many implications of Lasswell's basic hypothesis which we have not been able to consider here. Erik H. Erikson's *Young Man Luther* (New York: W. W. Norton & Co., 1959) explores the connection between Luther's personal crisis of identity and the broader European identity crisis of the Reformation period. Here, as in his *Childhood and Society* (New York: W. W. Norton & Co., 1963), Erikson provides life developmental concepts which nicely complement Lasswell's more psychodynamic approach.

Following one or the other of these precedents are a number of good studies of individual leaders. Alexander and Juliette George, *Woodrow Wilson and Colonel House* (New York: The John Day Co., 1956), is insightful, carefully researched, and a model of methodological self-consciousness. Lewis Edinger's *Kurt Schummacher* (Stanford, Calif.: Stanford University Press, 1965) emphasizes the interaction between Schummacher's compensatory needs and his adult political experiences. Arnold Rogow's *James Forrestal* (New York: The Macmillan Co., 1963) focuses on the role of Forrestal's psychopathology in the policy process. E. Victor Wolfenstein's *The Revolutionary Personality* (Princeton, N.J.: Princeton University Press, 1967) emphasizes the psychological factors that incline men to revolutionary participation and leadership.

Among the books that are psychoanalytically informed but not explicitly psychoanalytic, especial attention should be given to Fawn Brodie's *Thaddeus Stevens* (New York: W. W. Norton & Co., 1959).

Adherency. Here the classic study is T. W. Adorno, et al., *The Authoritarian Personality* (New York: Harper & Row, 1950). Incisive criticism of this pioneering effort is provided in Richard Christie and Marie Jahoda, eds., *Studies in the Scope and Method of "The Authoritarian Personality"* (Glencoe, Ill.: The Free Press, 1954). Erich Fromm's *Escape From Freedom* (New York: Holt, Rinehart & Winston, 1941) develops less rigorously, but more provocatively, the insights of these works.

The nature of political loyalty is dramatically explored in Nathan Leites' *The Ritual of Liquidation* (Glencoe, Ill.: The Free Press, 1954), an intensive analysis of the Stalinist purge trials. Gustav M. Gilbert, in *The Psychology of Dictatorship* (New York: Ronald Press, 1950), analyzes Hitlerism. Less extreme political adherency is explored in Robert Lane's *Political Ideology* (New York: The Free Press, 1962), a study of the political cognitions and emotions of the American common man. Fred I. Greenstein's *Children and Politics* (New Haven, Conn.: Yale University Press, 1965) studies the inculcation and ac-

ceptance of political beliefs in the American system. Martha Wolfenstein and Gilbert Kliman, *Children and the Death of a President*
(Garden City, N.Y.: Doubleday & Co., 1965), is also helpful in this
regard.

Political Philosophy.   There has been little systematic work in this
area. Lewis Feuer, *Psychoanalysis and Ethics* (Springfield, Ill.:
Charles C. Thomas, 1955), uses psychoanalytic theory to look at questions of values, and also examines the values inherent in psychoanalytic theory. Kurt Eissler's massive study, *Goethe* (Detroit: Wayne
State University Press, 1963, 2 vols.), and William Blanchard's
Rousseau and the Spirit of Revolt: A Psychological Study (Ann
Arbor, Mich.: University of Michigan Press, 1968) are good examples
of analyses of individual thinkers. Nathan Leites, *A Study of Bolshe-
vism* (Glencoe, Ill.: The Free Press, 1953) provides an exhaustive
treatment of the psychodynamics of Bolshevik ideology.

Index

✓. other Lasswell
Books   Psycho
Path.
✓ 2. Adorno   & Politics

✓ 3. Biographies

4. Rorschach

5. Orenstein

6. McCloskey

Miller & Stokes —
1958 Am. Repres.
Study ICPR
7226, 7292,
7293

No

Inter Univ
Consortium
For Polit
Research